CALIFORNIA INFORMATION GUIDES SERIES

Trade and Professional Associations in California: A Directory

SEVENTH EDITION

CALIFORNIA

INSTITUTE

OF PUBLIC

AFFAIRS

Telephone 916-442-CIPA (442-2472), Fax 916-442-2478
E-mail cipa@cipahq.org
Web site www.cipahq.org

See page 63 for information about the Institute. A complete list of publications is
available on request, or visit our Web site.

In obtaining the data contained herein, the editors have used information supplied to them by the
organizations listed and from other sources purporting to be accurate. However, neither the editors nor
the publisher can be held responsible for inaccuracies or omissions that may exist in this book.

First Edition, 1979; Second Edition, 1982; Third Edition, 1986; Fourth Edition, 1989; Fifth Edition,
1992; Sixth Edition, 1996; Seventh Edition, 1999

Library of Congress Cataloging-in-Publication Data

Trade and professional associations in California : a directory. –
  7th ed.
    p.   cm. – (California information guides series)
  Includes index.
  ISBN 1-880028-09-3
    1. Trade associations—California—Directories. 2. Professional
associations—California—Directories. I. California Institute of
Public Affairs. II. Series.
HD2428.C3T73 1999
061'.94'025—dc21   99-43206
                                                         CIP

Introduction

This is a directory of nonprofit business and professional associations located in California. It is limited to organizations of statewide or regional (northern or southern California) scope, national associations that have offices in the state, a few local groups of general interest, ethnic and binational chambers of commerce, and a few bistate trade associations. Local chambers of commerce are excluded.

Entries give the name of the organization and its address and telephone number. If there is more than one principal office in California, we have tried to list all of them. Listings are in alphabetical order and numbered. The **index** of subjects and key words, which begins on page 53, refers to entry numbers.

The seventh edition is thoroughly revised. Virtually all of the information given was verified by phone. As with past editions, organizations were identified through telephone directories, state lobbyist registration records, and the files of the California Institute of Public Affairs, which has a continuing program of collecting and disseminating information about California institutions.

Many other organizations concerned with the full range of California life—the environment, society, government, the economy, education, the arts, and history—are listed in *The California Handbook,* also published by CIPA.

No directory of this type is ever complete or, in spite of all pains taken, without errors. We urge users to contribute to the next edition by sending us additions and corrections.

Trade and Professional Associations A-Z Listing

-1-
Academy of Aphasia
c/o EBIRE
150 Muir Rd., 126S
Martinez, CA 94553
Requested phone not be listed

-2--
Academy of California Adoption Lawyers
16255 Ventura Blvd, Ste. 704
Encino, CA 91436
818-501-8355

-3-
Academy of Country Music
P.O. Box 508
Hollywood, CA 90028
323-462-2351

-4-
Academy of Motion Picture Arts and Sciences
8949 Wilshire Blvd.
Beverly Hills, CA 90211
310-247-3000

-5-
Academy of Television Arts and Sciences
5220 Lankershim Blvd.
North Hollywood, CA 91601
818-754-2800

-6-
Accordion Federation of North America, Inc.
11438 Elmcrest Street
El Monte, CA 91732
323-686-1769

-7-
Actors Fund of America
4727 Wilshire Blvd., Ste. 310
Los Angeles, CA 90010
323-933-9244

-8-
Adult Video Association
270 North Canon Drive, Ste. 1370
Beverly Hills, CA 90210
323-650-7121

-9-
Advertising Club of Los Angeles
6404 Wilshire Blvd., Ste. 1111
Los Angeles, CA 90048
323-782-1044

-10-
Advertising Club of San Diego
5625 Ruffin Road
San Diego, CA 92123
619-576-9833

-11-
Advertising Industry Emergency Fund
6404 Wilshire Blvd., Ste. 1111
Los Angeles, CA 90048
323-655-1951

-12-
Advertising Photographers of America
333 S. Beverly Drive
Beverly Hills, CA 90212
310-201-0781

-13-
Aerobics and Fitness Association of America
15250 Ventura Blvd., Ste. 200
Sherman Oaks, CA 91403
818-905-0040 or 800-446-2322

-14-
Agricultural Council of California
P.O. Box 1712
Sacramento, CA 95812
916-443-4887

-15-
Agricultural Energy Consumers Association
925 L Street, Ste. 800
Sacramento, CA 95814
916-447-6206

-16-
Air Conditioning and Refrigeration Contractors Association of Southern California
401 Shatto Place, Ste. 103
Los Angeles, CA 90020
323-738-7238

-17-
Air Transport Association of America
8939 South Sepulveda Blvd., Ste. 408
Los Angeles, CA 90045
310-670-5183

-18-
Alliance of American Insurers
332 Pine Street, Ste. 310
San Francisco, CA 94104
415-362-0870

-19-
Alliance of Black Entertainment Technicians
1869 Buckingham Road
Los Angeles, CA 90019
213-933-0746

-20-
Alliance of Motion Picture and TV Producers
15503 Ventura Blvd.
Encino, CA 91436
818-995-3600

-21-
Alliance of Western Milk Producers
1225 H Street, Ste. 102
Sacramento, CA 95814
916-447-9941

-22-
Allied Personal Communications Industries Association of California
925 L Street, Ste. 220
Sacramento, CA 95814
916-441-4166

-23-
Almond Board of California
1150 9th Street, Ste. 1500
Modesto, CA 95354
209-549-8262

-24-
American Academy of Dramatic Arts/West
300 N. Halstead Street
Pasadena, CA 91107
626-351-0551

-25-
American Academy of Fixed Prosthodontics
1930 Sea Way, P.O. Box 1409
Bodega Bay, CA 94923
707-875-3040

-26-

American Academy of
Medical Acupuncture
5820 Wilshire Blvd.,
Ste. 500
Los Angeles, CA 90036
323-937-5514
-27-
American Academy of
Ophthalmology
655 Beach Street
San Francisco, CA 94109
415-561-8500
-28-
American Academy of
Pain Management
13947 Mono Way
Sonora, CA 95370
209-533-9744
-29-
American Academy of
Pediatrics
3020 Childrens Way,
Mail Code 5005
San Diego, CA 92123
619-569-8816
-30-
American Academy of
Pediatrics
900 5th Avenue, Ste.
204
San Rafael, CA 94901
415-459-4775
-31-
American Advertising
Federation
251 Post Street
San Francisco, CA 94108
415-421-6867
-32-
American Agents
Alliance
260 S. Arroyo Parkway
Pasadena, CA 91105
626-795-0519
-33-
American Ambulance
Association
3800 Auburn Blvd., Ste.
C
Sacramento, CA 95821
916-483-3827
-34-
American Anaplastology
Association
493 8th Avenue
San Francisco, CA 94118
415-221-9775
-35-
American Architectural
Manufacturers
Association
1230 N Street
Sacramento, CA 95814
916-447-2262
-36-
American Association
for Artificial
Intelligence
445 Burgess Drive

Menlo Park, CA 94025
650-328-3123
-37-
American Association
for Career Education
2900 Amby Place
Hermosa Beach, CA 90254
310-376-7378
-38-
American Association
for Crystal Growth
P.O. Box 3233
Thousand Oaks, CA 91359
805-492-7047
-39-
American Association
for Medical
Transcription
3460 Oakdale Road, Ste.
M
Modesto, CA 95357
209-551-0883
-40-
American Association
for Pediatric
Ophthalmology and
Strabismus
P.O. Box 193832
San Francisco, CA 94119
415-561-8505
-41-
American Association
for the Advancement of
Science, Pacific
Division
California Academy of
Science, Golden Gate
Park
San Francisco, CA 94118
415-752-1554
-42-
American Association of
Advertising Agencies
130 Battery Street,
Ste. 330
San Francisco, CA 94111
415-291-4999
-43-
American Association of
Critical Care Nurses
101 Columbia
Aliso Viejo, CA 92656
949-362-2000
-44-
American Association of
Gynecological
Laparoscopists
13021 East Florence
Avenue
Santa Fe Springs, CA
90670
562-946-8774
-45-
American Association of
Mental Health
Professionals in
Corrections
P.O. Box 160208
Sacramento, CA 95816

916-323-8305
-46-
American Auto Racing
Writers and
Broadcasters
Association
922 North Pass Avenue
Burbank, CA 91505
818-842-7005
-47-
American Board of
Criminal Lawyers
693 Sutter Street, 5th
Floor
San Francisco, CA 94102
415-885-3100
-48-
American Board of
Podiatric Orthopedics
22910 Crenshaw Blvd.
Torrance, CA 90505
310-891-0100
-49-
American Buckskin
Registry Association
P.O. Box 3850
Redding, CA 96049
530-223-1420
-50-
American Business
Services Association
P.O. Box 1993
Rancho Cordova, CA
95741
916-658-0411
-51-
American Business
Women's Association
4881 Popeejoy Court
San Jose, CA 95118
408-978-6347
-52-
American Chemical
Society
2140 Shattuck Avenue,
Room 1101
Berkeley, CA 94704
510-848-0512
-53-
American Chemical
Society
14934 S. Figueroa
Street
Gardena, CA 90248
310-327-1216
-54-
American Cinema Editors
1041 North Formosa
West Hollywood, CA
90046
323-850-2900
-55-
American College for
Advancement in Medicine
23121 Verdugo Drive,
Ste. 204
Laguna Hills, CA 92653
949-583-7666
-56-

American College of
Cardiology, California
Chapter
13102 Laurinda Way
Santa Ana, CA 92705
714-744-3278
-57-
American College of
Chiropractic
Orthopedists
1030 Broadway, Ste. 101
El Centro, CA 92243
760-352-1452
-58-
American College of
Emergency Physicians
505 North Sepulveda
Blvd., Ste 12
Manhattan Beach, CA
90266
310-374-4039
-59-
American College of
Obstetricians and
Gynecologists
1409 Sutter Street
San Francisco, CA 94109
415-474-1818
-60-
American College of
Psychiatrists
732 Addison Street,
Ste. D
Berkeley, CA 94710
510-704-8020
-61-
American College of
Surgeons
5820 Wilshire Blvd.,
Ste. 500
Los Angeles, CA 90036
323-937-5514
-62-
American College of
Trial Lawyers
8001 Irvine Center
Drive, Ste. 960
Irvine, CA 92718
949-727-3194
-63-
American College of
Trust and Estate
Counsel
3415 S. Sepulveda
Blvd., Ste. 330
Los Angeles, CA 90034
310-398-1888
-64-
American Council of
Hypnotist Examiners
1147 East Broadway,
Ste. 340
Glendale, CA 91205
818-242-1159
-65-
American Council on
Exercise
5820 Oberlin Drive,
Ste. 102

San Diego, CA 92121
619-535-8227 or 800-
825-3636
-66-
American Criminal
Justice Association
3149 Clairidge Way
Sacramento, CA 95821
916-484-6553
-67-
American Desalting
Association
915 L Street, Ste. 1000
Sacramento, CA 95814
916-442-9285
-68-
American Down
Association (feathers)
3216 Eastwood Road
Sacramento, CA 95821
916-971-1135
-69-
American Electronics
Association
915 L Street, Ste. 1260
Sacramento, CA 95814
916-443-9059
-70-
American Electronics
Association
5201 Great America
Parkway, Ste. 520.
Santa Clara, CA 95054
408-987-4200
-71-
American Electronics
Association
4770 Campus Drive,
Suite 220
Newport Beach, CA 92660
949-477-5300
-72-
American Electronics
Association
10240 Flanders Court
San Diego, CA 92121
619-452-9288
-73-
American Fair Credit
Association
3517 Marconi Avenue,
Ste. 107B
Sacramento, CA 95821
916-482-5700
-74-
American Frozen Food
Institute
1838 El Camino Real,
Ste. 202
Burlingame, CA 94010
650-697-6835
-75-
American Film Marketing
Association
10850 Wilshire Blvd.,
9th Floor
Los Angeles, CA 90024
310-446-1000
-76-

American Handwriting
Analysis Foundation
P.O. Box 6201
San Jose, CA 95150
408-377-6775
-77-
American Harp Society
6331 Quebec Drive
Hollywood, CA 90068
323-463-0716
-78-
American Hypnosis
Association
18607 Vent Blvd., Ste.
310
Tarzana, CA 91356
818-758-2730
-79-
American Industrial
Real Estate Association
700 S. Flower Street,
Ste. 600
Los Angeles, CA 90017
213-687-8777
-80-
American Institute of
Aeronautics and
Astronautics
2221 Rosecrans Avenue,
Ste. 227
El Segundo, CA 90245
310-643-7510
-81-
American Institute of
Architects
130 Sutter Street, Ste.
600
San Francisco, CA 94104
415-362-7397
-82-
American Institute of
Architects
8687 Melrose Avenue,
Ste. M3
Los Angeles, CA 90069
310-785-1809
-83-
American Institute of
Architects
233 A Street, Ste. 200
San Diego, CA 92101
619-232-0109
-84-
American Institute of
Graphic Arts
116 The Plaza Pasadena
Pasadena, CA 91101
626-952-2442
-85-
American Institute of
Wine and Food
1550 Bryant Street,
Ste. 700
San Francisco, CA 94103
415-255-3000
-86-
American Insurance
Association

980 9th Street, Ste.
2060
Sacramento, CA 95814
916-442-7617
-87-
American Luggage
Dealers Association
1114 State Street, Ste.
316
Santa Barbara, CA 93101
805-966-6909
-88-
American Marketing
Association
San Francisco Bay Area
650-994-2429
-89-
American Medical Group
Association
3010 Old Ranch Parkway,
Ste. 205
Seal Beach, CA 90740
562-430-1191
-90-
American Mule
Association
264 Clovis Avenue
Clovis, CA 93612
559-324-6583
-91-
American Mustang
Association
P.O. Box 338
Yucaipa, CA 92399
805-946-8308
-92-
American Osteopathic
College of Occupational
and Preventive Medicine
PMB 246
5405 Alton Street, Ste.
5A
Irvine, CA 92604
949-653-8694
-93-
American Pancreatic
Association
24419 Denise Place
Newhall, CA 91321
805-259-0282
-94-
American Physical
Therapy Association,
California Chapter
2295 Gateway Oaks Drive
Sacramento, CA 95833
916-929-2782
-96-
American Planning
Association
1333 36th Street
Sacramento, CA 95816
916-736-2434
-97-
American Production and
Inventory Control
Society
3032 Bunker Hill Lane,
Ste. 202

Santa Clara, CA 95054
408-727-1125
-98-
American Seminar
Leaders Association
206 Sacramento Street,
Ste. 201
Nevada City, CA 95959
916-265-2685
-99-
American Sightseeing
International
490 Post Street, Ste.
1701A
San Francisco, CA 94102
415-986-2082
-100-
American Society for
Aesthetic Plastic
Surgery
11081 Winners Circle,
Ste. 200
Los Alamitos, CA 90720
562-799-2356
-101-
American Society for
Enology and Viticulture
P.O. Box 1855
Davis, CA 95617
530-753-3142
-102-
American Society for
Pediatric Neurosurgery
c/o J. Gordon McComb,
Neurosurgery,
1300 North Vermont
Avenue, Ste. 906
Los Angeles, CA 90027
323-663-8128
-103-
American Society for
Training and
Development
74 New Montgomery
Street, Ste. 230
San Francisco, CA 94105
415-979-0293
-104-
American Society of
Andrology
74 New Montgomery
Street, Ste. 230
San Francisco, CA 94105
415-764-4823
-105-
American Society of
Appraisers
1127 11th Street, Ste.
242
Sacramento, CA 95814
916-448-3381
-106-
American Society of
Association Executives
1730 I Street, Ste. 240
Sacramento, CA 95814
916-443-8980
-107-

American Society of
Cinematographers
1782 North Orange Drive
Hollywood, CA 90028
323-876-5080
-108-
American Society of
Civil Engineers
74 New Montgomery
Street, Ste. 230
San Francisco, CA 94105
415-546-6546
-109-
American Society of
Civil Engineers
1651 East 4th Street,
Ste. 244
Santa Ana, CA 92701
714-835-7912
-110-
American Society of
Composers, Authors, and
Publishers
7920 Sunset Blvd., Ste.
300
Los Angeles, CA 90047
323-883-1000
-111-
American Society of
Engineers and
Architects
511 Garfield Avenue
South Pasadena, CA
91030
323-682-1161
-112-
American Society of
Farm Managers and Rural
Appraisers
1127 11th Street, Ste.
242
Sacramento, CA 95814
916-448-3381
-113-
American Society of
Irrigation Consultants
P.O. Box 426
Byron, CA 94514
925-516-1124
-114-
American Society of
Landscape Architects,
California Council
3288 El Cajon Blvd.,
Ste. 4
San Diego, CA 92104
619-283-8818
-115-
American Society of
Mechanical Engineers
119C Paul Drive
San Rafael, CA 94903
415-499-1148
-116-
American Society of
Music Arrangers and
Composers
P.O. Box 11
Hollywood, CA 90078

323-658-5997
-117-
American Society of
Ocularists
493 8th Avenue
San Francisco, CA
941118
415-221-5765
-118-
American Society of
Ophthalmic Registered
Nurses
P.O. Box 193030
San Francisco, CA 94119
415-561-8513
-119-
American Society of
Plumbing Engineers
3617 Thousand Oaks
Blvd., Ste. 210
Westlake, CA 91362
805-495-7120
-120-
American Society of
Podiatric Executives
c/o California PMA,
2430 K Street, Ste. 200
Sacramento, CA 95816
916-448-0248
-121-
American Society of
Women Accountants
11686 Regio Drive
Dublin, CA 94568
415-974-9491
-122-
American Society on
Aging
833 Market Street, Ste.
511
San Francisco, CA 94103
415-974-9600
-123-
American Sports
Medicine
Association/Board of
Certification
660 West Duarte Road
Arcadia, CA 91007
626-445-1978
-124-
American Subcontractors
Association/Bay Area
117 Town and Country
Village, Ste. 329
San Jose, CA 95128
800-732-7677
-125-
American Teleservices
Association
4605 Lankershim Blvd.,
Ste. 824
North Hollywood, CA
91602
800-441-3335
-126-
American Tunaboat
Association
1 Tuna Lane

San Diego, CA 92101
619-233-6405
-127-
American Vineyard
Foundation
P.O. Box 414
Oakville, CA 94562
707-967-9307
-128-
American Water Works
Association,
California-Nevada
Section
1225 S. Bon View Avenue
Ontario, CA 91761
909-930-1200
-129-
Antique Appraisal
Association of America
11361 Garden Grove
Blvd.
Garden Grove, CA 92643
714-530-7090
-130-
Apartment and Motel
Association of
California
2515 Sonoma Street
Torrance, CA 90503
310-212-6660
-131-
Apartment Association
14550 Archwood Street
Van Nuys, CA 91405
818-374-3240
-132-
Apartment Association
of Greater Los Angeles
621 South Westmoreland
Ave
Los Angeles, CA 90005
213-384-4131
-133-
Apartment Owners
Association
15025 Oxnard Street,
2nd Fl.
Van Nuys, CA 91411
323-872-3348
-134-
Apartment Owners
Association
3550 Long Beach Blvd.,
Ste. D4
Long Beach, CA 90807
562-595-6700
-135-
Apartment Owners
Association of Southern
California
8880 Rio San Diego
Drive, 8th Fl.
San Diego, CA 92108
-136
Applied Technology
Council
555 Twin Dolphin Drive
Redwood City, CA 94065
650-595-1542

-137-
Apricot Producers of
California
2125 Wylie Drive, Ste.
2A
Modesto, CA 95355
209-524-0801
-138-
Armenian Business
Alliance of California
P.O. Box 25405
Los Angeles, CA 90025
310-472-4618
-139-
Artichoke Advisory
Board
P.O. Box 747
Castroville, CA 95012
831-633-4411
-140-
Asian American
Architects and
Engineers
3250 Wilshire Blvd.,
2nd floor
Los Angeles, CA 90010
213-386-0273
-141-
Asian American
Journalists Association
1765 Sutter Street,
Room 1000
San Francisco, CA 94115
415-346-2051
-142-
Asian American
Manufacturers
Association
Menlo Park, CA 94025
650-321-2262
-143-
Asian and Pacific
Americans in Higher
Education
926 J Street, Ste. 719
Sacramento, CA 95814
Requested phone not be
listed
-144-
Asian Business League
of San Francisco
233 Sansome Street,
Ste. 1108
San Francisco, CA 94104
415-788-4664
-145-
Asphalt Pavement
Association
13967 Highway 94, Ste.
200
Jamul, CA 91935
800-734-9996
-146-
Associated Builders and
Contractors
1127 11th Street, Ste.
544
Sacramento, CA 95814
916-447-3828

-147-
Associated Builders and
Contractors
11875 Dublin Blvd.,
Ste. 2C258
Dublin, CA 94568
925-829-9230
-148-
Associated Builders and
Contractors
4152 30th Street
San Diego, CA 92103
619-283-2211
-149-
Associated California
Loggers
555 Capitol Mall, Ste.
745
Sacramento, CA 95814
916-441-7940
-150-
Associated Credit
Bureaus of California
5667 Hansen Drive
Pleasanton, CA 94566
925-846-5396
-151-
Associated General
Contractors of
California
3095 Beacon Blvd.
West Sacramento, CA
95691
916-371-2422
-152-
Associated General
Contractors of
California
1350 Treat Blvd., Ste.
450
Walnut Creek, CA 94596
925-776-2054
-153-
Associated General
Contractors of
California
1255 Corporate Center
Drive, Ste. 100
Monterey Park, CA 91754
213-263-1500
-154-
Associated General
Contractors of
California
3324 State Street, Ste.
DD
Santa Barbara, CA 93105
805-682-6242
-155-
Associated Independent
Dairies of America
1112 Salmon Drive
Roseville, CA 95661
916-783-7473
-156-
Associated Produce
Dealers and Brokers of
Los Angeles

1601 East Olympic
Blvd., Building 300,
Ste. 312
Los Angeles, CA 90021
213-623-6293
-157-
Associated Roofing
Contractors of Northern
California
6020 Rutland Drive,
Ste. 11
Carmichael, CA 95608
916-334-8874
-158-
Associated Roofing
Contractors of the Bay
Area Counties
8301 Edgewater Drive
Oakland, CA 94621
510-635-8800
-159-
Associated Surplus
Dealers
2950 31st Street,
Ste.100
Santa Monica, CA 90405
310-396-6006
-160-
Associated Tile
Contractors of Southern
California
3850 Main Street
Culver City, CA 90232
310-838-7962
-161-
Association Academy of
Medical Acupuncture
5820 Wilshire Blvd.,
Ste. 500
Los Angeles, CA 90036
323-937-5514
-162-
Association for
Computer Operations
Management
742 East Chapman Avenue
Orange, CA 92866
714-997-7966
-163-
Association for
Corporate Growth
2975 Bowers Avenue
Santa Clara, CA 95051
408-567-9802
-164-
Association for
Correctional Research
and Information
Management
129 Rivara Circle
Sacramento, CA 95864
916-487-9334
-165-
Association for Equine
Sports Medicine
3579 E. Foothill Blvd.,
Ste. 288
Pasadena, CA 91107
909-869-4859

-166-
Association for
Humanistic Psychology
45 Franklin Street,
Ste. 315
San Francisco, CA 94102
415-864-8850
-167-
Association of Applied
Insect Ecologists
1008 10th Street, Ste.
549
Sacramento, CA 95814
916-441-5224
-168-
Association of Area
Business Publications
5820 Wilshire Blvd.
Ste. 500
Los Angeles, CA 90036
323-937-5514
-169-
Association of
Biological Collections
Appraisers
3493 Greenfield Place
Carmel, CA 93923
831-624-5677
-170-
Association of
California Cartridge
Remanufacturers
4521 Campus Drive, Ste.
206
Irvine, CA 92612
949-225-8233
-171-
Association of
California Community
College Administrators
2017 O Street
Sacramento, CA 95814
916-443-3559
-172-
Association of
California Construction
Managers
1130 K Street, Ste. 210
Sacramento, CA 95814
916-441-3300
-173-
Association of
California Energy
Officials
P.O. Box 3008
Berkeley, CA 94703
510-869-2759
-174-
Association of
California Health Care
Districts
P.O. Box 255668
Sacramento, CA 95865
916-971-8200
-175-
Association of
California Insurance
Companies
1121 L Street, Ste. 510

Sacramento, CA 95814
916-442-4581
-176-
Association of
California Life and
Health Insurance
Companies
1201 K Street, Ste.
1820
Sacramento, CA 95814
916-442-3648
-177-
Association of
California Neurologists
5380 Elvas Avenue
Sacramento, CA 95819
916-457-2236
-178-
Association of
California School
Administrators
1517 L Street
Sacramento, CA 95814
916-444-3216
-179-
Association of
California School
Administrators
4308 Park Blvd.
San Diego, CA 92103
619-295-2117
-180-
Association of
California School
Administrators
1575 Bayshore Highway
Burlingame, CA 94010
650-692-4300
-181-
Association of
California State
Attorneys and
Administrative Law
Judges
660 J Street, Ste. 480
Sacramento, CA 95814
916-442-2272
-182-
Association of
California State
University Professors
9010 Reseda Blvd., Ste.
224
Northridge, CA 91324
818-886-1196
-183-
Association of
California Surety
Companies
925 L Street, Ste. 220
Sacramento, CA 95814
916-441-4166
-184-
Association of
California Traffic
Safety Educators
23944 Hawthorne Blvd.,
Ste 200
Torrance, CA 90505

310-791-7975
-185-
Association of
California Urban School
Districts
1115 11th Street
Sacramento, CA 95814
916-446-0906
-186-
Association of
California Water
Agencies
910 K Street, Ste. 1000
Sacramento, CA 95814
916-441-4545
-187-
Association of
Chartered Certified
Accountants, American
Branch
1250 Long Beach Avenue,
Ste. 323
Los Angeles, CA 90021
213-489-3668
-188-
Association of Child
Victim Treatment
Centers
926 J Street, Ste. 710
Sacramento, CA 95814
916-446-4300
-189-
Association of
Christian Schools
International
9812 Old Winery Place,
Ste. 17
Sacramento, CA 95827
916-363-2235
-190-
Association of Cinema
and Video Laboratories
7095 Hollywood Blvd.,
Suite 751
Hollywood, CA 90028
-191-
Association of Cleaning
Employers
1533 Sierra Bonita
Placentia, CA 92670
714-993-5530
-192-
Association of
Community Mental Health
Agencies
66 Hurlbut Avenue, Ste.
205
Pasadena, CA 91105
626-403-0344
-193-
Association of Computer
Training Professionals
650-570-6096
-194-
Association of Defense
Counsel of Northern
California
833 Market Street, Ste.
805

San Francisco, CA 94103
415-543-1020
-195-
Association of Defense
Counsel of Southern
California
888 South Figueroa,
16th Floor
Los Angeles, CA 90017
213-683-3050
-196-
Association of Desktop
Publishers
3401-A 800 Adams Avenue
San Diego, CA 92116
619-563-9714
-197-
Association of
Educational Therapists
1804 W. Burbank Blvd.
Burbank, CA 91506
818-788-3850
-198-
Association of
Engineering Geologists
3037 Walkyne Way
Sacramento, CA 95821
916-928-3300
-199-
Association of
Engineering Geologists
898 Union Street
Alameda, CA 94501
510-353-0320
-200-
Association of
Engineering Geologists
6416 Woodley Avenue
Van Nuys, CA 91406
818-786-8884
-201-
Association of
Environmental
Professionals
1333 36th Street
Sacramento, CA 95816
916-737-2371
-202-
Association of
Independent California
Colleges and
Universities
1100 11th Street, Ste.
315
Sacramento, CA 95814
916-446-7626
-203-
Association of
Independent Colleges of
Art and Design
3957 22nd Street
San Francisco, CA 94114
415-642-8595
-204-
Association of Internet
Professionals
140 Second Street
San Francisco, CA 94105
415-243-8900

11

-205-
Association of Korean
Oriental Medicine and
Acupuncture of
California
3750 W. 6th Street
Los Angeles, CA 90020
213-382-4412
-206-
Association of Legal
Administrators
P.O. Box 19-2265
San Francisco, CA 94119
415-979-6880
-207-
Association of Low
Wealth Schools
925 L Street, Ste. 1400
Sacramento, CA 95814
916-448-2196
-208-
Association of Moving
Image Archivists
8949 Wilshire Blvd.
Beverly Hills, CA 90211
310-550-1300
-209-
Association of Naval
Aviation
Marine Corps Air
Station, El Toro
Santa Ana, CA 92630
562-431-3780
-210-
Association of
Osteopathic State
Executive Directors
455 Capitol Mall, Ste.
230
Sacramento, CA 95814
916-447-2004
-211-
Association of
Professional Design
Firms
P.O. Box 29166
San Francisco, CA 94129
415-626-9774
-212-
Association of
Professional Energy
Managers
143 South Citrus Street
Orange, CA 92868
213-481-5831 or 800-
543-3563
-213-
Association of Regional
Center Agencies
915 L Street, Ste. 1050
Sacramento, CA 95814
916-446-7961
-214-
Association of Reporter
Training Schools
7985 Santa Monica
Blvd., Ste. 398
West Hollywood, CA
90046

818-386-2424
-215-
Association of Reporter
Training Schools
1100 N Street, Ste. 2C
Sacramento, CA 95814
-216-
Association of Retired
Teachers
323-666-0544
-217-
Association of Rural
Northern California
Energy Providers
904 G Street
Eureka, CA 95501
707-444-3831
-218-
Association of Southern
California Defense
Counsel
888 South Figueroa
Street, 16th Floor
Los Angeles, CA 90017
213-683-3050
-219-
Association of Talent
Agents
9255 Sunset Blvd., Ste.
930
Los Angeles, CA 90069
310-274-0628
-220-
Association of
Technical Personnel in
Ophthalmology
P.O. Box 193940
San Francisco, CA 94119
800-482-4858
-221-
Association of Textile
Dyers, Printers, and
Finishers of Southern
California
2833 Leonis Blvd., Ste.
316
Los Angeles, CA 90058
323-589-5833
-222-
Association of Threat
Assessment
Professionals
2211 Corinth Avenue
Los Angeles, CA 90064
310-312-0212
-223-
Association of
University Professors
of Ophthamology
P.O. Box 420369
San Francisco, CA 94142
415-561-8548
-224-
Association of Winery
Suppliers
21 Tamal Vista Blvd.
Ste. 196
Corte Madera, CA 94925
414-924-2640

-225-
Astronomical Society of
the Pacific
390 Ashton
San Francisco, CA 94112
415-337-1100
-226-
Audio Publishers
Association
617 S. Aviation Way
Manhattan Beach, CA
90266
310-372-0546
-227-
Australian-American
Chamber of Commerce of
Southern California
611 North Larchmont
Blvd., 3rd Floor
Los Angeles, CA 90004
323-469-6316
-228-
Automatic Transmission
Rebuilders Association
2472 Eastman Avenue,
Ste. 23
Ventura, CA 93003
805-654-1700
-229-
Automotive
International
Association
P.O. Box 4910
Diamond Bar, CA 91765
909-396-0289
-230-
Automotive Repair
Coalition
915 L Street
Sacramento, CA 95814
916-444-9742
-231-
Automotive Service
Council
P.O. Box 19391
San Diego, CA 92159
619-544-0440
-232-
Automotive Service
Councils
758 University Ave
Sacramento, CA 95825
916-924-9054
-234-
Automotive Trade
Organizations
3002 Dow Avenue, Suite
308
Tustin, CA 92780
714-734-1801
-235-
Bar Association of San
Diego County (lawyers)
1333 7th Avenue
San Diego, CA 92101
619-231-0781
-236-
Bar Association of San
Francisco (lawyers)

465 California Street,
Ste. 1100
San Francisco, CA 94104
415-982-1600
-237-
Bay Area Advertising
Relief Committee
(provides emergency
financial aid to
members of the
advertising industry)
130 Battery Street,
Ste. 320
San Francisco, CA 94111
415-392-2272
-238-
Bay Area Book Reviewers
Association
c/o Joyce Jenkins,
Poetry Flash
1450 4th Street
Berkeley, CA 94710
510-525-5476
-239-
Bay Area Economic Forum
200 Pine Street
San Francisco, CA 94104
415-981-7117
-240-
Bay Area Entrepreneur
Association
977 East Stanley Blvd.,
Ste. 199
Livermore, CA 94550
925-806-8686
-241-
Bay Area League of
Industrial Associations
155 Jackson, Ste. 305
San Francisco, CA 94111
415-788-2739
-242-
Bay Area Organizational
Development Network
5 Third Street
San Francisco, CA 94103
415-777-5250
-243-
Biocom (formerly
Biomedical Industry
Council)
4510 Executive Drive,
Plaza 1
San Diego, CA 92121
619-455-0300
-244-
Biomedical Engineering
Society
P.O. Box 2399
Culver City, CA 90231
310-459-1999
-245-
Black Advocates in
State Service
1722 J Street, Ste. 16
Sacramento, CA 95814
916-492-2277
-246-

Black Data Processing
Associates
2625 Alcatraz Avenue,
Ste. 197
Berkeley, CA 94705
510-654-3807
-247-
Blue Diamond Growers
(also known as
California Almond
Growers)
1802 C Street
Sacramento, CA 95814
916-442-0771
-248-
Book Publicists of
Southern California
6464 Sunset Blvd., Ste.
580
Hollywood, CA 90028
323-461-3921
-249-
Bookbuilders West (book
production)
P.O. Box 7046
San Francisco, CA 94120
415-273-5790
-250-
British-American
Chamber of Commerce
1640 Fifth Street, Ste.
203
Santa Monica, CA 90401
310-394-4977
-251-
Builders Exchange
735 Industrial Road
San Carlos, CA 94070
650-591-4486
-252-
Builders Exchange
110 Belvedere Street
San Rafael, CA 94901
415-456-3233
-253-
Building Industry
Association
24005 Ventura Blvd.
Calbasas, CA 91302
818-591-2001
-254-
Building Industry
Credit and Supply
Coalition
1127 11th Street, Ste.
747
Sacramento, CA 95814
916-444-3770
-255-
Building Industry
Credit Association
2351 W. Third Street
Los Angeles, CA 90057
213-251-1179
-256-
Building Owners and
Managers Association
1730 I Street, Ste. 240
Sacramento, CA 95814

916-443-9092
-257-
Building Owners and
Managers Association
465 California Street,
Ste. 504
San Francisco, CA 94104
415-362-8567
-258-
Building Owners and
Managers Association
700 South Flower
Street, Ste. 2325
Los Angeles, CA 90017
213-629-2662
-259-
Building Owners and
Managers Association,
Los Angeles District
700 South Flower, Ste.
2329
Los Angeles, CA 90017
213-629-2662
-260-
Building Owners and
Managers Association,
San Jose District
63 Metro Drive
San Jose, CA 95110
408-453-7222
-261-
Bulgarian-American
Chamber of Commerce
6464 Sunset Blvd., Ste.
850
Los Angeles, CA 90028
323-962-2414
-262-
Business for Social
Responsibility
609 Mission Street
San Francisco, CA 94105
415-537-0888
-263-
Business Forum, The
9250 Wilshire Blvd.,
Ste. 220
Beverly Hills, CA 90212
310-550-1984
-264-
Business Marketing
Association
467 Saratoga Avenue,
Ste. 1205
San Jose, CA 95129
408-365-9815
-265-
Cal-Neva Community
Action Association
(organizations helping
low-income people)
225 30th Street, Ste.
200
Sacramento, CA 95816
916-443-1721
-266-
California Academy of
Child and Adolescence
Psychiatry

1400 K Street, Ste. 816
Sacramento, CA 95814
916-498-1622

-267-
California Academy of
Cosmetic Surgery
785 University Avenue
Sacramento, CA 95825
916-564-9999

-268-
California Academy of
Family Physicians
114 Sansome Street,
Ste. 1305
San Francisco, CA 94104
415-394-9121

-269-
California Academy of
Higher Education
7380 Parkway Drive
La Mesa, CA 91942
619-465-3990

-270-
California Academy of
Ophthalmology
605 Market Street, Ste.
1109
San Francisco, CA 94105
415-777-3937

-271-
California Academy of
Physician Assistants
3100 W. Warner Avenue,
Ste. 3
Santa Ana, CA 92704
714-427-0321

-272-
California Academy of
Vesselite Practitioners
Vesselite Center, 1-304
Sacramento, CA 95818-
9040

-273-
California Acupuncture
Medical Association
12751 Brockhurst Way
Garden Grove, CA 92841
714-638-2922

-274-
California Adult
Business Association
1808 Sherwood Avenue
Sacramento, CA 95822
916-456-7311

-275-
California Adult
Education
Administrators
Association
1331 E. Calaveras
Milpitas, CA 95035
408-945-2347

-276-
California Agricultural
Aircraft Association
2100 Flightline Drive,
Ste. 3
Lincoln, CA 95648
530-645-9747

-277-
California Agricultural
Commissioners and
Sealers Association
316 Nelson Street
Oroville, CA 95965
916-538-7381

-278-
California Agricultural
Production Consultants
Association
1143-W N. Market Blvd.
Sacramento, CA 95834
916-928-1625

-279-
California Agricultural
Teachers Association
1100 N Street, Ste. 1D
Sacramento, CA 95814
916-443-2282

-280-
California Air
Pollution Control
Officers Association
3232 Western Drive
Cameron Park, CA 95682
530-676-4323

-281-
California Alarm
Association
1541 Ocean Avenue, Ste.
200
Santa Monica, CA 90401
310-395-4349

-282-
California Ambulance
Association
3800 Auburn Blvd.
Sacramento, CA 95821
916-483-3852

-283-
California Ambulatory
Surgery Association
1 Capitol Mall, Ste.
320
Sacramento, CA 95814
707-578-4100

-284-
California Apartment
Association
980 9th Street, Ste.
2150
Sacramento, CA 95814
916-447-7881

-285-
California Appellate
Defense Counsel
Mailing address: 909
Marina Village Parkway,
Ste. 584
Alameda, CA 94501
619-295-4241

-286-
California Apple
Association
4974 E. Clinton Way,
Ste. 125
Fresno, CA 93727
559-456-0900

-287-
California Applicants'
Attorneys Association
801 12th Street, Ste.
201
Sacramento, CA 95814
916-444-5155

-288-
California Aquaculture
Association
P.O. Box 1004
Niland, CA 92257
760-359-3474

-289-
California Aquaculture
Association
3700 Chaney Court
Carmichael, CA 95608
916-944-7315

-290-
California-Arizona
Citrus League
25060 Ave. Stanford,
Ste. 200
Valencia, CA 91355
805-257-3682

-291-
California Artichoke
Advisory Board
P.O. Box 741
Castroville, CA 95012
831-633-4411

-292-
California Artichoke
and Vegetable Growers
10855 Caramia Parkway,
Ste. A
Castroville, CA 95012
831-633-2144

-293-
California Asparagus
Commission
4565 Quail Lakes Drive,
Ste. A1
Stockton, CA 95207
209-474-7581

-294-
California Assisted
Living Facilities
Association
455 Capitol Mall, Ste.
232
Sacramento, CA 95814
916-448-1900

-295-
California Association
for Bilingual Education
660 S. Figueroa Street,
Ste. 1040
Los Angeles, CA 90017
213-532-3850

-296-
California Association
for Counseling and
Development
2555 East Chapman
Avenue, Ste. 201
Fullerton, CA 92831
714-871-6460

-297-
California Association
for Health Care Quality
2818 E. Hamilton Avenue
Fresno, CA 93721
559-237-1660
-298-
California Association
for Health, Physical
Education, Recreation,
and Dance
1501 El Camino Avenue,
Ste. 3
Sacramento, CA 95815
916-922-3596
-299-
California Association
for Health Services at
Home
723 S Street
Sacramento, CA 95814
916-443-8055
-300-
California Association
for Medical Laboratory
Technology
1895 Mowry Avenue, Ste.
112
Fremont, CA 94538
510-792-4441
-301-
California Association
for Microenterprise
Opportunity
655 13th Street, Ste.
201
Oakland, CA 94621
510-238-8360
-302-
California Association
for Relocatable
Classrooms
5700 Las Positas
Livermore, CA 94550
510-276-2626
-303-
California Association
of Administrators of
State and Federal
Education Programs
9510 Elk Grove-Florin
Road
Elk Grove, CA 95624
916-686-7712
-304-
California Association
of Alcohol and Drug
Program Executives
1127 11th Street, Ste.
208
Sacramento, CA 95814
916-329-7409 or 800-
288-1222
-305-
California Association
of Alcoholic Recovery
Homes
5777 Madison Avenue,
Ste. 1210

Sacramento, CA 95841
916-338-9460
-306-
California Association
of Alcoholism and Drug
Abuse Counselors
3400 Bradshaw Road,
Ste. A5
Sacramento, CA 95827
916-368-9412
-307-
California Association
of Area Agencies on
Aging
980 9th Street, Ste.
700B
Sacramento, CA 95814
916-443-2800
-308-
California Association
of Auto Brokers
3339 West Temple Street
Los Angeles, CA 90026
818-501-2222
-309-
California Association
of Behavior Analysis
2220 Capitol Avenue
Sacramento, CA 95816
916-447-7341
-310-
California Association
of Bioanalysts
640 Glendale Terrace
Glendale, CA 91206
916-447-0193
-311-
California Association
of Black Social Workers
7100 S. Western Avenue
Los Angeles, CA 90047
213-752-9223
-312-
California Association
of Business Brokers
1608 West Campbell
Avenue, Ste. 248
Campbell, CA 95008
408-379-7748
-313-
California Association
of Catholic Hospitals
1121 L Street, Ste. 409
Sacramento, CA 95814
916-444-3386
-314-
California Association
of CD-ROM Producers
1808 Sherwood Avenue
Sacramento, CA 95822
916-456-7311
-315-
California Association
of Children's Homes
1431 3rd Street, Ste.
12
Sacramento, CA 95814
916-442-4800
-316-

California Association
of Collectors
P.O. Box 254490
Sacramento, CA 95865
916-929-2125
-317-
California Association
of Community Managers
18662 MacArthur Blvd.
Irvine, CA 92715
949-262-2226
-318-
California Association
of Councils of
Governments
1127 11th Street, Ste.
830
Sacramento, CA 95814
916-557-1170
-319-
California Association
of County Treasurers
and Tax Collectors
1029 J Street, Ste. 340
Sacramento, CA 95814
916-441-1850
-320-
California Association
of County Veterans
Service Officers
1300 South Grand
Avenue, Bldg. B
Santa Ana, CA 92705
714-567-7485
-321-
California Association
of Dental Managed Care
Organizations
1 Capitol Mall
Sacramento, CA 95814
916-446-3122
-322-
California Association
of Dental Plans
1 Capitol Mall
Sacramento, CA 95814
916-446-3122
-323-
California Association
of Dispensing
Physicians
7701 Fay Avenue
La Jolla, CA 92037
619-454-0033
-324-
California Association
of Drinking Driver
Treatment Programs
1014 11th Street, PMB
108
Sacramento, CA 95814
916-621-3597
-325-
California Association
of Employers (labor
relations)
10732 Riverside Drive
North Hollywood, CA
91602

818-760-4132
-326-

California Association
of Employers
1485 Response Road,
Ste. 107
Sacramento, CA 95815
916-921-1312
-327-

California Association
of Environmental Health
Administrators
3700 Chaney Court
Carmicheal, CA 95608
916-944-7315
-328-

California Association
of Farm Advisors and
Specialists
2145 West Wardrobe
Avenue
Merced, CA 95340
209-385-7403
-329-

California Association
of Harbor Masters and
Port Captains
P.O. Box 2098
Seal Beach, CA 90740
-330-

California Association
of Health Facilities
523 W. 6th Street
Los Angeles, CA 90014
213-627-3000
-331-

California Association
of Health Plans
1201 K Street
Sacramento, CA 95814
916-552-2910
-332-

California Association
of Health Underwriters
1225 8th Street
Sacramento, CA 95814
916-442-8831
-333-

California Association
of Highway Patrolmen
P.O. Box 161209
Sacramento, CA 95816
916-452-6751
-334-

California Association
of Homes and Services
for the Aging
7311 Greenhaven Drive,
Ste. 175
Sacramento, CA 95831
916-392-5111
-335-

California Association
of Ice Cream Vendors
11891 Mount Royal Court
Alta Loma, CA 91737
909-948-1083
-336-

California Association
of Independent
Accountants
1251 West Acacia
Hemet, CA 92543
800-894-8995
-337-

California Association
of Independent Business
P.O. Box 100
Claremont, CA 91711
909-445-0020
-338-

California Association
of Independent
Insurance Adjusters
P.O. Box 3159
Napa, CA 94558
707-258-2530
-339-

California Association
of Industrial Banks
1121 L Street, Ste. 100
Sacramento, CA 95814
916-329-9370
-340-

California Association
of Interlock Service
Providers
7545 Convoy Court
San Diego, CA 92111
619-637-3540
-341-

California Association
of Jail Educators
926 J Street, Ste. 816
Sacramento, CA 95814
916-448-9169
-342-

California Association
of Joint Powers
Authorities
530 Bercut Drive, Suite
G
Sacramento, CA 95814
916-325-0143
-343-

California Association
of Licensed
Investigators
908 21st Street
Sacramento, CA 95816
916-441-5444
-344-

California Association
of Licensed
Repossessors
P.O. Box 775
Fairfield, CA 94533
707-422-0993
-345-

California Association
of Licensed Security
Agencies, Guards, and
Associates
P.O. Box 2563
Elk Grove, CA 95759
916-684-8182
-346-

California Association
of Life Underwriters
770 L Street, Ste. 900
Sacramento, CA 95814
916-443-2788
-347-

California Association
of Lime Growers
P.O. Box 278
Fallbrook, CA 92088
760-728-4567
-348-

California Association
of Local Agency
Formation Commissions
P.O. Box 180
Salinas, CA 93902
831-755-5065
-349-

California Association
of Local Conservation
Corps
1371 Stanislaus Avenue
Fresno, CA 93706
559-264-1048
-350-

California Association
of Local Housing
Finance Agencies
1001 6th Street, Ste.
402
Sacramento , CA 95814
916-444-0288
-351-

California Association
of Managers and
Supervisors
11344 Coloma Road
Rancho Cordova, CA
95670
916-853-2446
-352-

California Association
of Marriage and Family
Therapists
7901 Raytheon Road
San Diego, CA 92111
619-292-2638
-353-

California Association
of Medical Directors
1721 Second Street
Sacramento, CA 95814
916-556-3355
-354-

California Association
of Medical Products
Suppliers
1 Capitol Mall, Ste.
320
Sacramento, CA 95814
916-443-2115
-355-

California Association
of Mortgage Brokers
1730 I Street, Ste. 240
Sacramento, CA 95814
916-448-8236
-356-

California Association
of Naturopathic
Physicians
112 Douglas Blvd.
Roseville, CA 95678
800-521-1200
-357-

California Association
of Neurological
Surgeons
5380 Elvas Avenue
Sacramento, CA 95819
916-457-2267
-358-

California Association
of Nonprofits
315 W. 9th Street, Ste.
705
Los Angeles, CA 90015
213-347-2070
-359-

California Association
of Nurse Anesthetists
237 E. Katella Avenue
Orange, CA 92867
714-744-0155
-360-

California Association
of Nurserymen
3947 Lennane Drive
Sacramento, CA 95834
916-928-3900
-361-

California Association
of Obstetricians and
Gynegologists
1110 2nd Street
Sacramento, CA 95814
916-446-1111
-362-

California Association
of Ophthalomogy
605 Market Street, Ste.
1109
San Francisco, CA 94105
415-777-3937
-363-

California Association
of Oral and
Maxillofacial Surgeons
151 N. Sunrise Avenue,
Ste. 1304
Roseville, CA 95661
916-783-1332
-364-

California Association
of Parliamentarians
2159 42nd Avenue
San Francisco, CA 94116
415-566-7826
-365-

California Association
of Photocopiers and
Process Servers
530 Bercut Drive, Ste.
G
Sacramento, CA 95814
916-444-8963
-366-

California Association
of Port Authorities
1510 14th Street
Sacramento, CA 95814
916-446-6339
-367-

California Association
of Private
Postsecondary Schools
629 J Street
Sacramento, CA 95814
916-447-5500
-368-

California Association
of Private Specialized
Education and Services
520 P Street, Ste. 23
Sacramento, CA 95814
916-447-7061
-369-

California Association
of Professional
Employer Organizations
1 Capitol Mall
Sacramento, CA 95814
916-444-3568
-370-

California Association
of Professional
Liability Insurers
1201 K Street, Ste. 190
Sacramento, CA 95914
916-448-9777
-371-

California Association
of Professional
Scientists
660 J Street, Ste. 480
Sacramento, CA 95814
916-441-2629
-372-

California Association
of Progressive Rental
Organizations
P.O. Box 1748
Suisun City, CA 94585
707-421-8771
-373-

California Association
of Psychiatric
Technicians
2000 O Street, Ste. 250
Sacramento, CA 95814
916-329-9140
-374-

California Association
of Public
Administrators and
Public Guardians
21423 Devonshire Street
Chatsworth, CA 91311
818-998-2125
-375-

California Association
of Public Hospitals and
Health Systems
2000 Center Street,
Ste. 308
Berkeley, CA 94704

510-649-7650
-376-

California Association
of Public Retirement
Systems
11344 Coloma Road
Rancho Cordova, CA
95670
916-853-2440
-377-

California Association
of Real Estate Brokers
525 S. Virgil Avenue
Los Angeles, CA 90020
323-739-8200
-378-

California Association
of Realtors
980 9th Street, Ste.
1430
Sacramento, CA 95814
916-444-2045
-379-

California Association
of Recreation and Park
Districts
P.O. Box 4599
Auburn, CA 95604
530-888-1813
-380-

California Association
of Regional
Occupational Centers
and Programs
1130 K Street, Ste. 210
Sacramento, CA 95814
916-441-3302
-381-

California Association
of Regional Poison
Centers
113 Baurer Circle
Folsom, CA 95630
916-983-1415
-382-

California Association
of Rehabilitation and
Reemployment
Professionals
P.O. Box 9049
Chico, CA 95927
530-895-1781
-383-

California Association
of Rehabilitation
Facilities
980 9th Street, Ste.
420
Sacramento, CA 95814
916-441-5844
-384-

California Association
of Resource
Conservation Districts
801 K Street, 13th
Floor
Sacramento, CA 95814
916-447-7237
-385-

California Association
of Sanitation Agencies
925 L Street, Ste. 1400
Sacramento, CA 95814
916-446-0388
-386-

California Association
of Scholars
1730 Martin Luther King
Jr Way
Berkeley, CA 94709
510-843-4957
-387-

California Association
of School Business
Officials
1531 I Street, Ste. 310
Sacramento, CA 95814
916-447-3783
-388-

California Association
of School Psychologists
and Psychometrists
1400 K Street, Ste. 311
Sacramento, CA 95814
916-444-1595
-389-

California Association
of Services for
Children
P.O. Box 2769
Sacramento, CA 95812
916-446-0241
-390-

California Association
of Small Employer
Health Plans
5800 S. Eastern Avenue
Los Angeles, CA 90040
323-728-9500
-391-

California Association
of State Hearing
Reporters
2424 Arden Way, Ste.
230
Sacramento, CA 95825
916-263-2726
-392-

California Association
of State Investigators
185 Berry Street, Ste.
5600
San Francisco, CA 94107
916-447-5262
-393-

California Association
of Suburban School
Districts
P.O. Box 477
Carmichael, CA 95609
916-971-7111
-394-

California Association
of Teachers of English
3714 Dixon Place
San Diego, CA 92107
619-644-8100
-395-

California Association
of Teachers of English
to Speakers of Other
Languages
5721 John Chaffey
Circle
Garden Grove, CA 92645
310-599-8023
-396-

California Association
of Temporary and
Staffing Services
P.O. Box 16686
Sacramento, CA 92176
619-280-3528
-397-

California Association
of Temporary Services
P.O. Box 16686
San Diego, CA 92176
619-280-3528
-398-

California Association
of Thoroughbred
Racetracks
1024 10th Street, Ste.
320
Sacramento, CA 95814
916-449-6820
-399-

California Association
of Vocational
Administrators
P.O. Box 213030
Stockton, CA 95213
209-468-9004
-400-

California Association
of Wheat Growers
P.O. Box 255545
Sacramento, CA 95865
916-925-5709
-401-

California Association
of Winegrape Growers
555 University Avenue
Sacramento, CA 95825
916-924-5370
-402-

California Association
of Work Experience
Educators
2706 Euclid
Hughson, CA 95326
209-883-2803
-403-

California Association
of Zoos and Aquariums
P.O. Box 120551
San Diego, CA 92112
619-685-3221
-404-

California Athletic
Trainers Association
1127 11th Street, Ste.
350
Sacramento, CA 95814
916-448-3444
-405-

California Attorneys
for Criminal Justice
4929 Wilshire Blvd.,
Ste. 68
Los Angeles, CA 90010
213-933-9414
-406-

California Authority of
Racing Fairs
1776 Tribute Road, Ste.
150
Sacramento, CA 95815
916-927-7223
-407-

California Auto Auction
Association
P.O. Box 73000
Rio Linda, CA 95676
916-991-5555
-408-

California Autobody
Association
1116 24th Street
Sacramento, CA 95814
916-448-5477
-409-

California Automatic
Fire Alarm Association
3401 Pacific Avenue,
Ste. 1C
Marina del Rey, CA
90292
310-899-9950
-410-

California Automatic
Vendors Council
16030 Ventura Blvd.,
Ste. 215
Encino, CA 91436
818-783-8363
-411-

California Automotive
Wholesalers Association
11160 Sun Center Drive
Rancho Cordova, CA
95670
916-635-9774
-412-

California Aviation
Business Association
1 Capitol Mall, Ste.
320
Sacramento, CA 95814
916-658-0250
-413-

California Avocado
Commission
1251 East Dyer Road,
Ste. 200
Santa Ana, CA 92705
714-558-6761
-414-

California Bail Agents
Association
1127 11th Street, Ste.
331
Sacramento, CA 95814
916-446-3038
-415-

California Bail
Insurance Group
925 L Street, Ste. 220
Sacramento, CA 95814
-416-
California Bankers
Association
1121 L Street, Ste.
1050
Sacramento, CA 95814
916-441-7377
-417-
California Bankers
Clearing House
Association
950 S. Grand Avenue
Los Angeles, CA 90015
323-896-0491
-418-
California Barber
College Association
2645 El Camino Ave
Sacramento, CA 95821
916-482-0871
-419-
California Bean Growers
Association
P.O. Box 786
Newman, CA 95360
209-862-2300
-420-
California Bean
Shippers Association
1521 I Street
Sacramento, CA 95814
916-441-2514
-421-
California Beauty
Supply Dealers
Association
519 W. Manchester
Avenue, Ste. 104
Los Angeles, CA 90044
323-752-1113
-422-
California Beef Council
5726 Sonoma Avenue
Pleasanton, CA 94566
925-484-2333
-423-
California Beer and
Beverage Distributors
Association
1 Capitol Mall, Ste.
230
Sacramento, CA 95814
916-441-5402
-424-
California Beet Growers
Association (sugar
beets)
2 West Swain Road
Stockton, CA 95207
209-477-5596
-425-
California Beverage
Merchants
1716 X Street
Sacramento, CA 95818

916-444-9800
-426-
California Biomedical
Research Association
P.O. Box 24-D-06
Los Angeles, CA 90024
310-268-8080
-427-
California Biomedical
Research Association
1008 10th Street, Ste.
328
Sacramento, CA 95814
916-558-1515
-428-
California Botanical
Society
Jepson Herbarium
University of
California, 1001 VLSB,
Rm. 2465
Berkeley, CA 94720
510-643-7008
-429-
California Broadcasters
Association
1127 11th Street, Ste.
400
Sacramento, CA 95814
916-444-2237
-430-
California Building
Industry Association
1107 9th Street, Ste.
1060
Sacramento, CA 95814
916-443-7933
-431-
California Building
Industry Foundation
3800 Watt Avenue, Ste.
138
Sacramento, CA 95821
916-959-4850
-432-
California Building
Officials
2215 21st Street
Sacramento, CA 95818
916-457-1103
-433-
California Bus
Association
11020 Commercial Park
Way
Castroville, CA 95012
800-664-2877
-434-
California Business
Alliance
777 Campus Commons
Road, Ste. 200
Sacramento, CA 95825
916-565-7691
-435-
California Business and
Restaurant Alliance
2265 Westwood Blvd.,
Suite 481

Los Angeles, CA 90064
310-474-7919
-436-
California Business
Properties Association
1121 L Street, Ste. 809
Sacramento, CA 95814
916-443-4676
-437-
California Cable
Television Association
P.O. Box 11080
Oakland, CA 94611
510-428-2225
-438-
California Canning
Peach Association
P.O. Box 7001
Lafayette, CA 94549
510-284-9171
-439-
California Canteloupe
Advisoy Board
531 N. Alta Avenue
Dinuba, CA 93618
559-591-5715
-440-
California Cast Metals
Association
1011 St. Andrews Drive,
Ste. I
El Dorado Hills, CA
95762
916-933-3062
-441-
California Cattlemen's
Association
1221 H Street
Sacramento, CA 95814
916-444-0845
-442-
California Cement
Producers Coalition
3633 Inland Empire
Blvd., Ste. 900
Ontario, CA 91764
909-466-5900
-443-
California Cement
Promotion Council
263 West El Pintado
Road
Danville, CA 94526
925-838-0701
-444-
California Certified
Organic Farmers
1115 Mission Street
Santa Cruz, CA 95060
831-423-2263
-445-
California Chamber of
Commerce
(Note: Local chambers
of commerce are not
included in this
directory, except for
ethnic organizations.
For a list of local

chambers, contact the California Chamber of Commerce)
1201 K Street, 12th Fl.
Sacramento, CA 95814
916-444-6670
-446-
California Chamber of Commerce, Agricultural Committee
P.O. Box 1736
Sacramento, CA 95812
916-444-6670
-447-
California Check Cashers Association
1716 X Street
Sacramento, CA 95818
916-448-5220
-448-
California Cheese and Butter Association
911 Ventura Way
Mill Valley, CA 94941
415-381-6791
-449-
California Cherry Advisory Board
P.O. Box 877, Lodi, CA 95240
209-368-0685
-450-
California Children's Hospital Association
1620 5th Avenue, Ste. 725
San Diego, CA 92101
619-232-1674
-451-
California Chiropractic Association
1600 Sacramento Inn Way
Sacramento, CA 95815
916-648-2727
-452-
California Christmas Tree Growers Association
8608 Washington Road
Hilmar, CA 95324
800-454-8733
-453-
California Chrysanthemum Growers Association
788 San Antonio Road
Palo Alto, CA 94303
650-494-1451
-454-
California Cigar Association
1015 20th Street
Sacramento, CA 95814
916-448-0529
-455-
California Cleaners Association
1730 I Street, Ste. 240
Sacramento, CA 95814

916-443-0986
-456-
California Cling Peach Growers Advisory Board
531 N. Alta Avenue
Dinuba, CA 93618
209-595-1425
-457-
California Clinical Laboratory Association
1127 11th Street, Ste. 820
Sacramento, CA 95814
916-446-2646
-458-
California Coalition of Nurse Practitioners
27369 Eagle View Court
El Macero, CA 95618
530-756-7555
-459-
California Coalition of Travel Organizations
925 L Street, Ste. 220
Sacramento, CA 95814
916-441-4166
-460-
California Community College Football Coaches Association
1499 North State Street
San Jacinto, CA 92583
909-654-8011, ext. 1562
-461-
California Compensation Defense Attorneys Association
P.O. Box 161057
Sacramento, CA 95816
916-442-3686
-462-
California Concrete Contractors Association
P. O. Box 5547
Napa, CA 94581
707-224-0222
-463-
California Confederation of the Arts
704 O Street, 2nd Floor
Sacramento, CA 95814
916-447-7811
-464-
California Conference of Arson Investigators
1122 East Lincoln Avenue, Ste. 202
Orange, CA 92865
714-283-2295
-465-
California Congress of Parents, Teachers, and Students
930 Georgia Street
Los Angeles, CA 90015
213-620-1100
-466-

California Construction Advancement Program
2215 21st Street
Sacramento, CA 95818
916-736-9389
-467-
California Continuation Education Association
P.O. Box 1029
Pollock Pines, CA 95726
530-644-1895
-468-
California Contract Security Guard Association
7770 Pardee Lane
Oakland, CA 94621
510-568-0276
-469-
California Corn Growers
P.O. Box 726
Chowchilla, CA 93610
209-665-5775
-470-
California Correctional Peace Officers Association
755 River Point Drive, Ste. 200
West Sacramento, CA 95605
916-372-6561
-471-
California Cosmetology Coalition
1100 N Street, Ste. 5E
Sacramento, CA 95814
916-442-4344
-472-
California Cotton Ginners Association
1941 North Gate Way, Ste. 101
Fresno, CA 93727
559-252-0684
-473-
California Cotton Growers Association
1941 North Gateway Blvd., Ste. 101
Fresno, CA 93727
559-252-0684
-474-
California Council for Adult Education
1006 4th Street, Ste. 260
Sacramento, CA 95814
916-444-3323
-475-
California Council for Interior Design Certification
1605 Grand Avenue, Ste. 4
San Marcos, CA 92069
760-761-4734
-476-

California Council for
International Trade
580 Washington Street,
Ste. 305
San Francisco, CA 94111
415-788-4127
-477-
California Council for
the Social Studies
P.O. Box 902470
Palmdale, CA 93590
805-533-2277
-478-
California Council of
Churches
2700 L Street
Sacramento, CA 94816
916-442-5447
-479-
California Council of
Community Mental Health
Agencies
1127 11th Street, Ste.
830
Sacramento, CA 95814
916-557-1166
-480-
California Court Clerks
Association
P.O. Box 38
San Leandro, CA 94577
510-553-0401
-481-
California Court
Reporters Association
2400 22nd Street, Ste.
110
Sacramento, CA 95814
916-443-5090
-482-
California Creamery
Operators Association
313 Casa Linda Drive
Woodland, CA 95695
530-662-1228
-483-
California Credit Union
League
1121 L Street, Ste. 410
Sacramento, CA 95814
916-443-7935
-484-
California Crop
Improvement Association
c/o Parsons Seed
Certification Center
University of
California
Davis, CA 95616
530-752-0544
-485-
California Cut Flower
Commission
73 Hangar Way
Watsonville, CA 95076
831-728-7333
-486-
California Dairy Herd
Improvement Association

150 Clovis Avenue, Ste.
102
Clovis, CA 93612
209-323-2600
-487-
California Dairy
Research Foundation
502 Mace Blvd.
Davis, CA 95616
530-753-0681
-488-
California Date
Administrative
Committee
P.O. Box 1736
Indio, CA 92202
760-347-4510
-489-
California Date
Commission
45701 Monroe Street,
Ste. H
Indio, CA 92201
760-347-4510
-490-
California Defense
Counsel
1107 9th Street
Sacramento, CA 95814
916-447-3508
-491-
California Dental
Assistants Association
5100 N. 6th Street
Fresno, CA 93710
559-227-4220
-492-
California Dental
Association
1201 K Street
Sacramento, CA 95814
916-443-0505
-493-
California Dental
Hygienists Association
660 J Street, Ste. 480
Sacramento, CA 95814
916-442-4531
-494-
California Dental
Laboratory Association
39111 Paseo Padre
Parkway, Ste. 213
Fremont, CA 94538
510-745-9677
-495-
California Department
of Forestry Employees
Association
(CDF firefighters)
924 Enterprise Drive
Sacramento, CA 95825
916-641-2096
-496-
California Deposition
Agency Owners and
Reporters Association
249 N. Brand Blvd.,
Ste. 806

Glendale, CA 91203
818-551-7300
-497-
California Dermatology
Society
1127 11th Street
Sacramento, CA 95814
916-498-1712
-498-
California Desert Grape
Administrative
Committee
82-365 Highway 111,
Ste. 108
Indio, CA 92201
760-342-4385
-499-
California Dietetic
Association
7740 Manchester Avenue,
Ste. 102
Playa del Rey, CA 90293
310-822-0177
-500-
California Distributors
Association
(formerly California
Association of Tobacco
and Candy Distributors)
925 L Street, Ste. 300
Sacramento, CA 95814
916-446-7841
-501-
California District
Attorneys Association
731 K Street, Ste. 300
Sacramento, CA 95814
916-443-2017
-502-
California Drum
Reconditioners Task
Force
1051 Union Street
Montebello, CA 90640
323-724-8500
-503-
California Dry Bean
Advisory Board
531 N. Alta Avenue,
Ste. D
Dinuba, CA 93618
559-591-4866
-504-
California Dump Truck
Owners Association
334 North Euclid Avenue
Upland, CA 91786
909-982-9898
-505-
California Egg
Commission
1150 N. Mountain
Avenue, Ste. 114
Upland, CA 91786
909-981-4923
-506-
California Elected
Women's Association for
Education and Research

CSUS, 6000 J Street
Sacramento, CA 95819
916-278-3870
-507-
California Electric
Sign Association
29170 Heather Cliff
Road, Ste. 6
Malibu, CA 90265
310-457-8375
-508-
California Emissions
Testing Industries
Association
1024 10th Street
Sacramento, CA95814
916-443-6714
-509-
California Employee
Pharmacist Association
6363 Wilshire Blvd.,
Ste. 215
Los Angeles, CA 90048
323-655-5532
-510-
California Engineering
Foundation
2700 Zinfandel Drive
Rancho Cordova, CA
95670
916-853-1914
-511-
California Escrow
Association
530 Bercut Drive, Ste.
G
Sacramento, CA 95814
916-325-0600
-512-
California Fabricare
Institute Association
1730 I Street, Ste. 240
Sacramento, CA 95814
916-443-0986
-513-
California Faculty
Association (faculty in
the California State
University system)
400 Capitol Mall, Ste.
1950
Sacramento, CA 95814
916-441-4848
-514-
California Farm Bureau
Federation
2300 River Plaza Drive
Sacramento, CA 95833
916-561-5500
-515-
California Fashion
Association
110 E. 9th Street, Ste.
C-277
Los Angeles, CA 90079
213-688-6288
-516-

California Federation
of Business and
Professional Women
1459 Gemini Court
Bakersfield, CA 93309
661-837-8291
-517-
California Fence
Contractors Association
1534 Genesis Court
Rohnert Park, CA 94928
707-585-1795
-518-
California Fertilizer
Association
1700 I Street, Ste. 130
Sacramento, CA 95814
916-441-1584
-519-
California Fig Advisory
Board
3425 North First
Street, Ste. 109
Fresno, CA 93726
559-224-3447
-520-
California Fig
Institute
3425 North First
Street, Ste. 109
Fresno, CA 93726
559-224-3447
-521-
California Film
Extruders and
Convertors Association
2402 Vista Nobleza
Newport Beach, CA 92660
949-640-9901
-522-
California Financial
Services Association
980 9th Street, Ste.
2160
Sacramento, CA 95814
916-446-1207
-523-
California Financial
Service Providers
1716 X Street
Sacramento, CA 95814
800-775-5220
-524-
California Fire Chiefs
Association
825 M Street
Rio Linda, CA 95673
916-991-0293
-525-
California Fisheries
and Seafood Institute
1521 I Street
Sacramento, CA 95814
916-441-5560
-526-
California Floral
Council
P.O. Box 925
Half Moon Bay, CA 94019

650-726-5299
-527-
California Forest
Products Commission
853 Lincoln Way, Ste.
208
Auburn, CA 95603
530-823-2363
-528-
California Forestry
Association
300 Capitol Mall, Ste.
350
Sacramento, CA 95814
916-444-6592
-529-
California Freestone
Peach Association
1704 Herndon Road
Ceres, CA 95307
209-538-2372
-530-
California Fresh Carrot
Advisory Board
531D North Alta Avenue
Dinuba, CA 93618
209-591-5675
-531-
California Funeral
Directors Association
347 Main Street
Placerville, CA 95667
800-255-2332
-532-
California Funeral
Directors Association
1 Capitol Mall, Ste.
320
Sacramento, CA 95814
916-325-2361
-533-
California Fuyu Growers
Association
(persimmons)
P.O. Box 1301
Valley Center, CA 92082
760-749-3359
-534-
California Golfcourse
Superintendents
Association
10928 Caminito Street
San Diego, CA 92131
619-566-3400
-535-
California Grain and
Feed Association
1521 I Street
Sacramento, CA 95814
916-441-2272
-536-
California Grape and
Tree Fruit League
(grower labor
relations)
1540 East Shaw Avenue,
Ste. 120
Fresno, CA 93710
209-226-6330

-537-
California Grocers
Association
P.O. Box 2671
Sacramento, CA 95812
916-448-3545
-538-
California Groundwater
Association
P.O. Box 14369
Santa Rosa, CA 95402
707-578-4408
-539-
California Grower
Foundation (farm labor
relations)
1108 Adams Street
St. Helena, CA 94574
707-963-7191
-540-
California Harness
Horse Breeders
Association
P.O. Box 54767
Sacramento, CA 95865
916-263-7888
-541-
California Hazardous
Waste Association
717 K Street. Ste. 500
Sacramento, CA 95814
916-447-7571
-542-
California Healthcare
Association
(hospitals and health
systems)
1201 K Street
Sacramento, CA 95814
916-443-7401
-543-
California Health
Information Association
5108 East Clinton Way,
Ste. 113
Fresno, CA 93727
559-251-5038
-544-
California Hispanic
Chambers of Commerce
343 E. Main Street,
Ste. 701
Stockton, CA 95202
209-547-1337
-545-
California Hotel and
Motel Association
P.O. Box 160405
Sacramento, CA 95816
916-444-5780
-546-
California Housing
Authorities Association
1001 6th Street, Ste.
402
Sacramento, CA 95814
916-444-0288
-547-

California Housing
Council
1225 8th Street, Ste.
550
Sacramento, CA 95814
916-447-3353
-548-
California Incontinent
Product Suppliers
Association
725 30th Street, Ste.
102
Sacramento, CA 95816
916-447-9999
-550-
California Independent
Oil Marketers
Association
3831 N. Freeway Blvd.
Sacramento, CA 95834
916-646-5999
-551-
California Independent
Petroleum Association
1112 I Street, Ste. 350
Sacramento, CA 95814
916-447-1177
-552-
California Institute
for Mental Health
1119 K Street, 2nd
Floor
Sacramento, CA 95814
916-556-3480
-553-
California Institute
for Professional
Investigators
140 Encinitas Blvd.,
Ste. 440
Encinitas, CA 92024
800-400-7448
-554-
California Institute,
Trade Association
Office
517 19th Street
Sacramento, CA 95814
916-442-2475
-555
California Insurance
Guarantee Association
8383 Wilshire Blvd.
Beverly Hills, CA 90211
213-782-0252
-556-
California Insurance
Wholesalers Association
3601 Haven Avenue
Menlo Park, CA 94025
650-780-4800
-557-
California Internet
Service Providers
1112 I Street, Ste. 101
Sacramento, CA 95814
916-431-7989
-558-

California Intractable
Pain Association
338 S. Glendora
West Covina, CA 91790
626-919-4798
-559-
California Judges
Association
301 Howard Street, Ste.
1040
San Francisco, CA 94105
415-495-1999
-560-
California Kiwifruit
Commission
9845 Horn Road
Sacramento, CA 95827
916-362-7490
-561-
California Land
Surveyors Association
P.O. Box 9098
Santa Rosa, CA 95405
707-578-6016
-562-
California Land Title
Association
1110 K Street, Ste. 100
Sacramento, CA 95814
916-444-2647
-563-
California Landscape
Contractors Association
2021 N Street, Ste. 300
Sacramento, CA 95814
916-448-2522
-564-
California Law
Enforcement Association
of Records Supervisors
c/o CSU Chico Police
Dept.
Chico, CA 95929
530-898-5372
-565-
California Lawyers for
the Arts
Fort Mason Center,
Building C, Room 255
San Francisco, CA 94123
415-775-7200
-566-
California League of
Food Processors
660 J Street, Ste. 290
Sacramento, CA 95814
916-444-9260
-567-
California League of
High Schools
18012 Cowan, Ste. 110
Irvine, CA 92614
949-253-7474
-568-
California League of
Middle Schools
18012 Cowan, Ste. 110
Irvine, CA 92614
949-261-2567

-569-
California Legislative
Conference of the
Plumbing, Heating, and
Piping Industry
1127 11th Street, Ste.
747
Sacramento, CA 95814
916-443-3114
-570-
California Legislative
Conference on Interior
Design
915 L Street, Ste. 100
Sacramento, CA 95814
916-444-2440
-571-
California Legislative
Council of Professional
Engineers
1127 11th Street, Ste.
242
Sacramento, CA 95814
916-448-3111
-572-
California Library
Association
717 K Street, Ste. 300
Sacramento, CA 95814
916-447-8541
-573-
California Licensed
Beverage Association
10866 Wilshire Blvd.
Los Angeles, CA 90024
310-475-7242
-574-
California Licensed
Foresters Association
P.O. Box 1516
Pioneer, CA 95666
209-293-7323
-575-
California Licensed
Vocational Nurses
Association
716 19th Street
Sacramento, CA 95814
916-483-0426
-576-
California Limousine
Association
1210 Cyprus Avenue
San Mateo, CA 94401
415-344-4400
-577-
California Locksmiths
Association
1240 N. Jefferson
Street
Anaheim, CA 92807
800-767-5625
-578-
California Lodging
Industry Association
2020 Hurley Way, Ste.
390
Sacramento, CA 95825
916-925-2915

-579-
California Macadamia
Society
P.O. Box 1298
Fallbrook, CA 92088
760-743-0358
-580-
California Manufactured
Housing Institute
10630 Town Center
Drive, Ste. 120
Rancho Cucamonga, CA
91730
909-987-2559
-581-
California
Manufacturers
Association
980 9th Street, Ste.
2200
Sacramento, CA 95814
916-441-5420
-582-
California
Manufacturing Milk
Advisory Board
3800 Cornucopia Street,
Ste. D
Modesto, CA 95380
209-525-6875
-583-
California Marine
Affairs and Navigation
Conference
813 Harbor Blvd., Ste.
290
West Sacramento, CA
95691
702-747-2243
-584-
California Marine Parks
and Harbors Association
40 San Leandro Marina
San Leandro, CA 94577
510-297-5197
-585-
California Media and
Library Educators
Association
Changed name to
California School
Library Association,
which see
-586-
California Medical
Association
1201 K Street, Ste.
1050
Sacramento, CA 95814
916-444-5532
-587-
California Medical
Association
P.O. Box 7690
San Francisco, CA 94120
415-541-0900
-588-

California Medical
Transportation
Association
P.O. Box 296
San Bruno, CA 94066
650-877-8250
-589-
California Mental
Health Directors
Association
1119 K Street, 2nd
Floor
Sacramento, CA 95814
916-556-3477
-590-
California Mining
Association
1 Capitol Mall, Ste.
220
Sacramento, CA 95814
916-447-1977
-591-
California Mobilehome
Parkowners Alliance
924 Westwood Blvd.,
Ste. 910
Los Angeles, CA 90024
310-208-0075
-592-
California Mortgage
Association
530 Bercut Drive, Ste.
G
Sacramento, CA 95814
916-325-0601
-593-
California Mortgage
Banker Association
980 9th Street, Ste.
1450
Sacramento, CA 95814
916-446-7100
-594-
California Mortuary
Alliance
1116 24th Street
Sacramento, CA 95816
916-448-5551
-595-
California Mosquito and
Vector Control
Association
8633 Bond Road
Elk Grove, CA 95624
916-685-2600
-596-
California Motorcar
Dealers Association
420 West Culver Blvd.
Playa del Rey, CA 90293
310-306-6232
-597-
California Moving and
Storage Association
4281 Katella Avenue,
Ste. 205
Los Alamitos, CA 90720
714-527-7866
-598-

California Municipal
Utilities Association
1225 8th Street, Ste.
440
Sacramento, CA 95814
916-441-1733
-599-
California Mutual Water
Companies Association
7452 Dufferin Avenue
Riverside, CA 92504
909-780-1333
-600-
California Narcotic
Officers' Association
28245 Ave. Crocker,
Ste. 230
Valencia, CA 91355
661-775-6960
-601-
California Nevada
Hereford Association
P.O. Box 56
Vinton, CA 96135
530-993-4216
-602-
California Nevada Soft
Drink Association
1 Capitol Mall, Ste.
320
Sacramento, CA 95814
916-443-6900
-603-
California Newspaper
Publishers Association
1225 8th Street, Ste.
260
Sacramento, CA 95814
916-443-5991
-604-
California Nurses
Association
1100 11th Street, Ste.
200
Sacramento, CA 95814
916-446-5019
-605-
California Nurses
Association
2000 Franklin Street,
Ste. 300
Oakland, CA 94612
510-273-2200
-606-
California Nurses
Association
3250 Ocean Park Blvd.
Santa Monica, CA 90405
-607-
California Nurses
Association
3611 5th Avenue
San Diego, CA 92103
619-297-6233
-608-
California Nurses for
Ethical Standards
4521 N. Sultana Avenue
Rosemead, CA 91770

310-558-1760
-609-
California Olive
Association
660 J Street, Ste. 290
Sacramento, CA 95814
916-444-9260
-610-
California Olive
Committee
1903 North Fine Avenue,
Ste. 102
Fresno, CA 93727
209-456-9096
-611-
California Optical
Laboratories
Association
17300 17th Street, Ste.
J306
Tustin, CA 92680
714-730-6380
-612-
California Optometric
Association
P.O. Box 2591
Sacramento, CA 95812
916-441-3990
-613-
California Organization
of Police and Sheriffs
301 E. Olive Avenue
Burbank , CA 91502
818-841-2222
-614-
California Orthopaedic
Association
5380 Elvas Avenue, Ste.
221
Sacramento, CA 95819
916-454-9884
-615-
California Ostrich
Association
P.O. Box 7464
Stockton, CA 95267
-616-
California Paint
Council
1333 36th Street
Sacramento, CA 95816
916-454-5435
-617-
California Park and
Recreation Society
7971 Freeport Blvd.
Sacramento, CA 95832
916-665-2777
-618-
California Parks
Hospitality Association
2150 Main Street
Red Bluff, CA 96080
530-529-1572
-619-
California Peace
Officers Association
1455 Response Drive,
Suite 190

Sacramento, CA 95816
916-263-0541
-620-
California Peach
Association
2300 River Plaza Drive
Sacramento, CA 95833
916-925-9131
-621-
California Pear
Advisory Board
1521 I Street
Sacramento, CA 95814
916-441-0432
-622-
California Pear Growers
4600 Northgate Blvd.
Sacramento, CA 95834
916-924-0530
-623-
California Pecan
Growers Association
18411 Fisher Drive
Visalia, CA 93292
559-592-7149
-624-
California Pepper
Commission
531D North Alta Avenue
Dinuba, CA 93618
559-591-3925
-625-
California Pharmacists
Association
1112 I Street, Ste. 300
Sacramento, CA 95814
916-444-7811
-626-
California Physicians
Alliance
560 20th Street
Oakland, CA 94612
510-832-7134
-627-
California Pilots
Association
P.O. Box 429
San Carlos, CA 94070
916-658-0250
-628-
California Pistachio
Commission
1318 East Shaw Avenue,
Ste. 420
Fresno, CA 93710
559-221-8294
-629-
California Plum
Marketing Board
P.O. Box 968
Reedley, CA 93654
559-638-8260
-630-
California Plumbing and
Mechanical Contractors
Association
370 Amapola Avenue,
Ste. 203
Torrance, CA 90501

310-381-3040

-631-
California Plumbing
Contractors Safety
Association
1911 F Street
Sacramento, CA 95814
916-448-1150

-632-
California Podiatric
Medical Association
2430 K Street, Ste. 200
Sacramento, CA 95816
916-448-0248

-633-
California Police
Chiefs' Association
1455 Response Road,
Ste. 190
Sacramento, CA 95815
916-253-0545

-634-
California Pork
Producers
P.O. Box 1800
Atascadero, CA 93423
805-461-5347

-635-
California Poultry
Industry Federation
3117A McHenry Avenue
Modesto, CA 95350
209-576-6355

-636-
California Precast
Concrete Association
Sacramento
916-362-1327

-637-
California Premium
Finance Association
1000 Q Street, Ste. 230
Sacramento, CA 95814
916-446-5165

-638-
California Primary Care
Association
1201 K Street
Sacramento, CA 95814
916-440-8170

-639-
California Probation,
Parole, and
Correctional
Association
211 Lathrop Way, Ste. M
Sacramento, CA 95815
916-927-4888

-640-
California Processing
Tomato Advisory Board
P.O. Box 980067
West Sacramento, CA
95798
916-371-3470

-641-
California Producer-
Handler Association
313 Casa Linda Drive

Woodland, CA 95695
530-662-1228

-642-
California Prune Board
5990 Stoneridge Drive,
Ste. 101
Pleasanton, CA 94588
925-734-0150

-643-
California Psychiatric
Association
1400 K Street, Ste. 302
Sacramento, CA 95814
916-442-5196

-644-
California
Psychological
Association
1022 G Street
Sacramento, CA 95814
916-325-9786

-645-
California Public
Defenders Association
3273 Ramos Circle
Sacramento, CA 95827
916-362-1686

-646-
California Public
Parking Association
1023 J Street, Ste. 202
Sacramento, CA 95814
916-264-7475

-647-
California Public
Securities Association
231 Apollo Way
Pleasant Hill, CA 94523
925-945-6498

-648-
California Public
Securities Association
P.O. Box 2531
San Francisco, CA 94126
925-945-6498

-649-
California Radiological
Society
1 Capitol Mall, Ste.
320
Sacramento, CA 95814
916-446-2028

-650-
California Rare Fruit
Growers
11261 Davenport Road
Los Alamitos, CA 90720

-651-
California Recreation
Vehicle Dealers
Association
1 Capitol Mall
Sacramento, CA 95814
916-658-0260

-652-
California
Redevelopment
Association
1400 K Street, Ste. 204

Sacramento, CA 95814
916-448-8760

-653-
California Redwood
Association
405 Enfrente Drive,
Ste. 200
Novato, CA 94949
415-382-0662

-654-
California Refuse
Removal Council
1121 L Street, Ste. 505
Sacramento, CA 95814
916-444-2772

-655-
California
Rehabilitation
Association
980 9th Street
Sacramento, CA 95814
916-441-5844

-656-
California Reserve
Peace Officers
Association
P.O. Box 5622
San Jose, CA 95150
408-371-8239

-657-
California Resource
Recovery Association
3031 F Street
Sacramento, CA 95816
916-441-2722

-658-
California Restaurant
Association
980 9th Street, Ste.
1480
Sacramento, CA 95814
916-447-5793

-659-
California Restaurant
Association
1620 5th Avenue, Suite
94
San Diego, CA 92101
619-230-0763

-660-
California Retail
Merchants Association
1000 Q Street
Sacramento, CA 95814
916-446-5165

-661-
California Retailers
Association
980 9th Street, Ste.
2100
Sacramento, CA 95814
916-443-1975

-662-
California Retired
Teachers Association
800 Howe Avenue, Ste.
370
Sacramento, CA 95825
916-923-2200

-663-
California Rice
Industry Association
701 University Avenue,
Ste. 205
Sacramento, CA 95825
916-929-3996

-664-
California Rice
Promotion Board
701 University Avenue,
Ste. 205
Sacramento, CA 95825
916-929-2264

-665-
California Roofers
Alliance
8 Corporate Park, Ste.
130
Irvine, CA 92714
949-476-1970

-666-
California Rural Water
Association
8300 Fair Oaks Blvd.
Carmichael, CA 95608
916-944-0236

-667-
California Salmon
Council
P.O. Box 2255
Folsom, CA 95763
916-358-2960

-668-
California School
Boards Association
3100 Beacon Blvd.
West Sacramento, CA
95691
916-371-4691

-669-
California School Bus
Contractors Association
1340 Treat Blvd., Ste.
210
Walnut Creek, CA 94596

-670-
California School
Employees Association
1127 11th Street, Ste.
346
Sacramento, CA 95814
916-444-0598

-671-
California School Food
Service Association
1804 W. Burbank Blvd.
Burbank, CA 91506
818-842-3040

-672-
California School Food
Service Association
3070 Kerner Blvd., Ste.
N
San Rafael, CA 94901
415-453-6325

-673-
California School
Library Association

1499 Old Bayshore
Highway, Ste. 142
Burlingame, CA 94010
650-692-2350

-674-
California School
Nurses Organization
926 J Street, Ste. 816
Sacramento, CA 95814
916-448-5752

-675-
California Science
Teachers Association
3550 Watt Avenue
Sacramento, CA 95821
916-979-7004

-676-
California Seafood
Council
P.O. Box 91540
Santa Barbara, CA 93190
805-568-3811

-677-
California Seed
Association
1521 I Street
Sacramento, CA 95814
916-441-2251

-678-
California Self
Insurers Association
921 11th Street, Ste.
619
Sacramento, CA 95814
916-442-4576

-679-
California Separation
Science Society
375 Alabama Street
San Francisco, CA 94110
415-487-9876

-680-
California Service
Station and Automotive
Repair Association
1202 Grant Avenue, Ste.
B1
Novato, CA 94945
415-892-1243

-681-
California Sheet Metal
and Air Conditioning
Contractors, National
Association
1020 12th Street, Ste.
101
Sacramento, CA 95814
916-442-3807

-682-
California Shortline
Railroad Association
1127 11th Street, Ste.
242
Sacramento, CA 95814
916-447-6006

-683-
California Ski Industry
Association

74 New Montgomery
Street, Ste. 750
San Francisco, CA 94105
415-543-7036

-684-
California Small
Business Association
P.O. Box 661235
Los Angeles, CA 90066
310-306-4540

-685-
California Small
Brewers Association
1330 21st Street, Ste.
201
Sacramento, CA 95814
916-444-8333

-686-
California Small
Business Alliance
413 Josefa Street
San Jose, CA 95126
408-995-0500

-687-
California Society for
Clinical Social Work
720 Howe Avenue, Ste.
112
Sacramento, CA 95825
916-923-0255

-688-
California Society for
Oriental Medicine
12926 Riverside Drive,
Ste. B
Sherman Oaks, CA 91423
818-789-2468

-689-
California Society for
Respiratory Care
925 L Street, Ste. 850
Sacramento, CA 95814
916-448-6802

-690-
California Society of
Anesthesiologists
1065 East Hillsdale
Blvd., Ste. 410
Foster City, CA 94404
650-345-3020

-691-
California Society of
Association Executives
1414 K Street, Suite
660
Sacramento, CA 95814
916-443-8980

-692-
California Society of
Certified Public
Accountants
1201 K Street, Ste.
1000
Sacramento, CA 95814
916-441-5351

-693-
California Society of
Certified Public
Accountants

3300 North Brand Blvd., Ste. 710
Glendale, CA 91203
818-246-6000
-694-
California Society of Enrolled Agents (tax preparers)
3200 Ramos Circle
Sacramento, CA 95827
916-366-6646
-695-
California Society of Health-System Pharmacists
725 30th Street, Ste. 208
Sacramento, CA 95816
916-447-1033
-696-
California Society of Industrial Medicine and Surgery
1000 Q Street
Sacramento, CA 95814
916-446-4199
-697-
California Society of Internal Medicine
P.O. Box 880606
San Francisco, CA 94188
415-882-5198
-698-
California Society of Oriental Medicine
12926 Riverside Drive, Ste. B
Sherman Oaks, CA 91423
818-789-2468
-699-
California Society of Pathologists
1 Capitol Mall, Ste. 320
Sacramento, CA 95814
916-446-6001
-700-
California Society of Plastic Surgeons
3664 San Pablo Dam Road
El Sobrante, CA 94803
510-243-1662
-701-
California Society of Professional Engineers
910 Florin Road, Ste. 112
Sacramento, CA 95831
916-422-7788
-702-
California Solar Energy Industries Association
21 Amador Circle
Rio Vista, CA 94571
949-837-7430
-703-
California Southeast Asia Business Council

1946 Embarcadero Street, Ste. 200
Oakland, CA 94606
510-536-1967
-704-
California Spa and Pool Industry Energy Codes and Legislative Council
980 9th Street, Ste. 430
Sacramento, CA 95814
916-447-4113
-705-
California Space and Technology Alliance
2225 Skyway Drive
Santa Maria, CA 93455
805-349-2633
-706-
California Special Districts Association
1121 L Street, Ste. 508
Sacramento, CA 95814
916-442-7887
-707-
California Speech-Language-Hearing Association
825 University Avenue
Sacramento, CA 95825
916-921-1568
-708-
California Speech Pathologists and Audiologists in Private Practice
825 University Avenue
Sacramento, CA 95825
916-921-1568
-709-
California State Association of Occupational Health Nurses
4151 Prospect Avenue
Los Angeles, CA 90027
209-847-6296
-710-
California State Association of Public Administrators, Public Guardians, and Public Conservators
20 North San Pedro Road, Ste. 2014
San Rafael, CA 94903
415-499-6187
-711-
California State Auctioneers Association
800-552-0220
-712-
California State Beekeepers Association
567 Edith Court
Santa Rosa, CA 95401
707-568-6549
-713-

California State Club Association
538 South Flower Street
Los Angeles, CA 90071
213-622-1391
-714-
California State Coroners' Association
5925 Maybrook Circle
Riverside, CA 92506
925-803-7899
-715-
California State Employees Association
1108 O Street
Sacramento, CA 95814
916-444-8134
-716-
California State Employees Association
2020 Challenger Drive, Ste. 102
Alameda, CA 94501
510-522-4357
-717-
California State Firefighters Association
2701 K Street
Sacramento, CA 95814
916-446-9880
-718-
California State Floral Association
1521 I Street
Sacramento, CA 95814
916-448-5266
-719-
California State Foster Parent Association
7545 Pratt Avenue
Citrus Heights, CA 95610
916-726-1960
-720-
California State Grange (farmers)
2101 Stockton Blvd.
Sacramento, CA 95817
916-454-5805
-721-
California State Horsemen's Association
P.O. Box 1228
Clovis, CA 93613
559-325-1055
-722-
California State Hospice Association
P.O. Box 160087
Sacramento, CA 95816
916-441-3770
-723-
California State Management Association
4920 Freeport Blvd., Ste. A
Sacramento, CA 95822
916-736-0606

-724-
California State
Outdoor Advertising
Association
925 L Street, Ste. 300
Sacramento, CA 95814
916-446-7843
-725-
California State
Sheriffs Association
2125 19th Street, Ste.
103
Sacramento, CA 95818
916-448-4242
-726-
California State
Society of Orthodontics
1323 Columbus Avenue,
Ste. 301
San Francisco, CA 94133
415-441-4697
-727-
California Stone Fruit
Coalition
4572 Avenue 400
Dinuba, CA 93618
209-897-7700
-728-
California Strawberry
Commission
P.O. Box 269
Watsonville, CA 95077
831-724-1301
-729-
California Surety
Federation
980 9th Street, Ste.
1580
Sacramento, CA 95814
916-447-8300
-730-
California Swap Meet
Association
120 N. Robertson Blvd.
Los Angeles, CA 90048
310-657-8420
-731-
California Sweet Potato
Growers Association
P.O. Box 534
Livingston, CA 95334
209-394-7935
-732-
California Table Grape
Commission
P.O. Box 5498
Fresno, CA 93704
559-224-4997
-733-
California Teachers
Association
1118 10th Street
Sacramento, CA 95814
916-442-5895
-734-
California Teachers
Association
1705 Murchison Drive
Burlingame, CA 94010

650-697-1400
-735-
California Teachers
Association
5757 W. Centory Blvd.,
Ste. 805
Los Angeles, CA 90045
310-642-6622
-736-
California Telephone
Association
1851 Heritage Lane,
Ste. 255
Sacramento, CA 95815
916-567-6700
-737-
California Thoracic
Society
202 Fashion Lane
Tustin, CA 92780
714-730-1944
-738-
California Thoroughbred
Breeders Association
201 Colorado Place
Arcadia, CA 91007
626-445-7800
-739-
California Thoroughbred
Trainers
P.O. Box 660039
Arcadia, CA 91066
626-446-0169
-740-
California Tire Dealers
and Retreaders
Association (see
Western States Tire and
Automotive Service
Association)
-741-
California Tomato
Commission
1625 E. Shaw Avenue
Fresno, CA 93711
559-251-0628
-742-
California Tomato
Growers Association
P.O. Box 7398
Stockton, CA 95267
209-478-1761
-743-
California Tow Trucking
Association
4121 Redwood Avenue
Los Angeles, CA 90066
310-306-7946
-744-
California Traffic
School Association
28780 Front Street,
Ste. B10
Temecula, CA 92590
909-695-4664
-745-
California Transit
Association (public
transportation)

1414 K Street, Ste. 320
Sacramento, CA 95814
916-446-4656
-746-
California Travel
Industry Association
1730 I Street, Ste. 240
Sacramento, CA 95814
916-443-3703
-747-
California Travel Parks
Association
P.O. Box 5648
Auburn, CA 95604
530-885-1624
-748-
California Trucking
Association
3251 Beacon Blvd.
West Sacramento, CA
95691
916-373-3500
-749-
California Trustees'
Association
530 Bercut Drive, Ste.
G
Sacramento, CA 95814
916-325-9911
-750-
California Urban Water
Agencies
455 Capitol Mall, Ste.
705
Sacramento, CA 95814
916-552-2929
-751-
California Union of
Safety Employees
2029 H Street
Sacramento, CA 95814
916-447-5262
-752-
California Urological
Association
1950 Old Tustin Avenue
Santa Ana, CA 92705
714-550-9194
-753-
California Veterinary
Medical Association
5231 Madison Avenue
Sacramento, CA 95841
916-344-4985
-754-
Western Wall and
Ceiling Contractors
Association
2286 N. State College
Blvd.
Fullerton, CA 92831
714-256-1244
-755-
California Walnut
Commission
1540 River Park Drive,
Ste. 203
Sacramento, CA 95815
916-646-3807

-756-
California Warehouse
Association
1521 I Street
Sacramento, CA 95814
916-441-1149
-757-
California Water
Association
12510 Fall Creek Lane
Cerritos, CA 90703
562-404-1993
-758-
California Water
Environmental
Association
7677 Oakport Street,
Ste. 525
Oakland, CA 94621
510-382-7800
-759-
California Wheat
Commission
P.O. Box 2267
Woodland, CA 95776
530-661-1292
-760-
California Wild Rice
Program
335 Teagarden Street
Yuba City, CA 95991
530-673-1927
-761-
California Women for
Agriculture
2818 E. Hamilton
Fresno, CA 93721
559-237-2474
-762-
California Women in
Timber
P.O. Box 993958
Redding, CA 96089
530-547-4303
-763-
California Women
Lawyers
926 J Street, Ste. 905
Sacramento, CA 95814
916-441-3703
-764-
California Wool Growers
Association
1225 H Street
Sacramento, CA 95814
916-444-8122
-765-
California Workers
Compensation Institute
120 Montgomery Street
San Francisco, CA 94104
415-981-2107
-766-
California Writers Club
2214 Derby Street
Berkeley, CA 94705
-767-

California-Nevada
Polled Hereford
Association
8500 Rock Springs Road
Penryn, CA 95663
916-663-1142
-768-
California-Nevada Soft
Drink Association
1 Capitol Mall, Ste.
320
Sacramento, CA 95814
916-443-6900
-769-
Canadian American
Chamber of Commerce
P.O. Box 2931
San Francisco, CA 94126
415-296-0961
-770-
Cantaloupe Advisory
Board
531D North Alta Avenue
Dinuba, CA 93618
209-591-5715
-771-
Car and Truck Renting
and Leasing Association
1228 N Street, Ste. 6
Sacramento, CA 95814
916-441-5858
-772-
Career Planning and
Adult Development
Network
4965 Sierra Road
San Jose, CA 95132
408-559-4946
-773-
Cellular Carriers
Association of
California
1225 8th Street, Ste.
550
Sacramento, CA 95814
916-553-5810
-774-
Ceramic Tile Institute
of America
12061 West Jefferson
Blvd.
Culver City, CA 90230
310-574-7800
-775-
Certified Alfalfa Seed
Council
P.O. Box 1017
Davis, CA 95617
530-752-0572
-776-
Certified Milk Product
Association of America
8300 Pine Avenue
Chino, CA 91710
909-393-0960
-777-
Chefs' Association of
the Pacific Coast

1550 Bryant Street,
Ste. 810
San Francisco, CA 94103
415-864-5627
-778-
Chemical Industry
Council of California
1765 Challenge Way
Sacramento, CA 95815
916-564-9394
-779-
Chief Probation
Officers Association of
California
1414 K Street, Ste. 660
Sacramento, CA 95814
916-340-1904
-780-
Chinese American
Association of Commerce
778 Clay Street, Ste. A
San Francisco, CA 94108
415-362-4306
-781-
Chinese Bay Area
Apparel Contractors
Association
950 Stockton Street,
Ste. 402
San Francisco, CA 94108
415-989-1907
-782-
Chinese Chamber of
Commerce
730 Sacramento Street
San Francisco, CA 94108
415-982-3000
-783-
Chinese Chamber of
Commerce of Los Angeles
977 North Broadway,
Ste. E
Los Angeles, CA 90012
213-617-0396
-784-
Christian Educators
Association
1550 East Elizabeth,
Ste. M-7
Pasadena, CA 91104
626-798-1124
-785-
City and Regional
Magazine Association
5820 Wilshire Blvd.,
Ste. 500
Los Angeles, CA 90036
323-937-5514
-786-
City Clerks Association
of California
1400 K Street
Sacramento, CA 95814
916-444-7505
-787-
Coalition of California
Independent Refiners
and Terminals

801 South Grand Avenue,
10th Floor
Los Angeles, CA 90017
213-624-8407
-788-
Coalition of Concerned
Legal Professionals
590 Leland Avenue
San Francisco, CA 94134
415-587-4240
-789-
Coalition of Concerned
Legal Professionals
3714 Marysville Blvd.
Sacramento, CA 95838
916-925-7994
-790-
Coalition of Concerned
Medical Professionals
2205 14th Avenue
Oakland, CA 94606
510-436-8020
-791-
Coalition of Prison-
Impacted Schools
1130 K Street, Ste. 210
Sacramento, CA 95814
916-441-3300
-792-
Collateral Loan and
Secondhand Dealers
Association
31 Post Street,
San Jose, CA 95113
408-295-1488
-793-
Commercial Financial
Conference of
California
626 Santa Monica Blvd.,
Ste. 129
Santa Monica, CA 90401
310-395-5073
-794-
Community Associations
Institute
1081 Camino del Rio
South
San Diego, CA 92108
619-299-1376
-795-
Community Bankers of
California
24050 Madison Street
Torrance, CA 90505
310-375-6302
-796-
Community College
Journalism Association
3376 Hill Canyon Avenue
Thousand Oaks, CA 91360
805-492-4440
-797-
Community College
League of California
2017 O Street
Sacramento, CA 95814
916-444-8641
-798-

Community Financial
Service Providers
Association
17019 Kingsview Avenue
Carson, CA 90746
310-538-2242
-799-
Community Residential
Care Association of
California
P.O. Box 163270
Sacramento, CA 95816
916-455-0723
-800-
Compact Flash
Association
P.O. Box 51537
Palo Alto, CA 94303
650-843-1220
-801-
Concrete Masonry
Association of
California and Nevada
6060 Sunrise Vista
Drive, Ste. 1990
Citrus Heights, CA
95610
916-722-1700
-802-
Conservation Committee
of California Oil and
Gas Producers
5300 Lennox Avenue,
Ste. 302
Bakersfield, CA 93309
805-635-0556
-803-
Construction Industry
Crime Prevention
1012 S Street
Sacramento, CA 95814
916-443-8796
-804-
Construction Industry
Legislative Council
1 Capitol Mall, Ste.
320
Sacramento, CA 95814
916-658-0250
-805-
Construction Industry
Research Board
2511 Empire Avenue
Burbank, CA 91504
818-841-8210
-806-
Construction Materials
Association of
California
1029 J Street, Ste. 300
Sacramento, CA 95814
916-554-1000
-807-
Construction
Specifications
Institute
493 8th Avenue
San Francisco, CA 94118
415-221-2170

-808-
Consulting Engineers
and Land Surveyors of
California
1303 J Street, Ste. 370
Sacramento, CA 95814
916-441-7991
-809-
Consumer Attorneys of
California (formerly
California Trial
Lawyers Association)
980 9th Street, Ste.
200
Sacramento, CA 95814
916-442-6902
-810-
Consumer Attorney
Association of Los
Angeles
3435 Wilshire Blvd.,
Ste. 2820
Los Angeles, CA 90010
213-487-1212
-811-
Consumer Attorneys of
San Diego
1305 7th Avenue, Ste.
110
San Diego, CA 92101
619-696-1166
-812-
Consumer Products
Council
P.O. Box 16907
Irvine, CA 92623
949-730-2791
-813-
Contractors Cooperative
Council
7077 Orangewood Avenue,
Ste. 120
Garden Grove, CA 92641
714-898-0583
-814-
Contractors Council of
California
601 University Avenue
Sacramento, CA 95825
916-923-9900
-815-
Cotton Incorporated
110 East 9th Street,
Ste. A703
Los Angeles, CA 90079
213-627-3561
-816-
Council of Acupuncture
and Oriental Medicine
Association
5363 Balboa Blvd., Ste.
234
Encino, CA 91316
818-788-4220
-817-
Council of California
County Law Librarians
515 North Flower Street
Santa Ana, CA 92703

714-834-3397

-818-

Council of University
of California Faculty
Associations
P.O. Box 33336
Grenada Hills, CA 91394
818-341-8664

-819-

County Alcohol and Drug
Program Administrators
Association of
California
1029 J Street, Ste. 340
Sacramento, CA 95814
916-441-1850

-820-

County Health
Executives Association
of California
1100 K Street, Ste. 101
Sacramento, CA 95814
916-327-7540

-821-

County Recorders'
Association of
California
25 County Center Drive
Chico, CA 95965
530-538-7691

-822-

County Welfare
Directors Association
1010 11th Street, Ste.
310
Sacramento, CA 95814
916-443-1749

-823-

Crab Boat Owners
Association
2907 Jones Street
San Francisco, CA 94133
415-885-1180

-824-

Crane Certification
Association of America
8810 Pierce Drive
Buena Park, CA 90620
714-828-8022

-825-

Credit Union Marketing
Association of
California
74 New Montgomery
Street
San Francisco, CA 94105
415-764-4848

-826-

Custom Upholsterers and
Decorators Association
6138 West Pico Blvd.
Los Angeles, CA 90035
323-852-4723

-827-

Customs Brokers and
Forwarders Association
of Northern California
1946 Embarcadero, Ste.
200

Oakland, CA 94606
510-536-2233

-828-

Customs Brokers and
Forwarders Association
of Northern California
P.O. Box 26269
San Francisco, CA 94126
510-536-2233

-829-

Dairy Council of
California
1101 National Drive,
Ste. B
Sacramento, CA 95834
916-263-3560

-830-

Dairy Institute of
California
1127 11th Street, Ste.
718
Sacramento, CA 95814
916-441-6921

-831-

Data Processing
Management Association
P.O. Box 5658
Buena Park, CA 90622
714-647-1617

-832-

Dental Laboratory
Owners Association of
California
333 Glendale Blvd.,
Ste. 4
Los Angeles, CA 90039
323-661-2188

-833-

Deposition Reporters of
California
1000 Q Street
Sacramento, CA 95814
916-446-2447

-834-

Diamond Walnut Growers
P.O. Box 1727
Stockton , CA 95201
209-467-6000

-835-

Dichondra Council
P.O. Box 1428
Woodland, CA 95776
530-666-3331

-836-

Direct Marketing
Association, Northern
California Chapter
4135 Blackhawk Plaza
Circle
Danville, CA 94506
925-648-4660

-837-

Direct Marketing Club
of Southern California
627 Aviation Way
Manhattan Beach, CA
90266
310-374-7499

-838-

Directors Guild of
America
7920 Sunset Blvd.
Los Angeles, CA 90046
310-289-2000

-839-

Diving Equipment and
Marketing Association
2050 Santa Cruz, Ste.
1000
Anaheim, CA 92805
714-939-6399

-840-

Dried Fruit Association
of California (dried
fruits and nuts)
1855 S. Van Ness Avenue
Fresno, CA 93704
559-233-7249

-841-

Driving School
Association of
California
28780 Front Street,
Ste. B10
Temecula, CA 92590
909-695-4664

-842-

Dry Bean Advisory Board
531 North Alta Avenue,
Rm. D
Dinuba, CA 93618
559-591-4866

-843-

Electric and Gas
Industries Association
P.O. Box 1938
San Leandro, CA 94577
510-357-6231

-844-

Electric Vehicle
Association of the
Americas
601 California Street
San Francisco, CA 94108
415-249-2690

-845-

Electrical Contractors
Association of
California
1127 11th Street, Ste.
832
Sacramento, CA 95814
916-444-3770

-846-

Electrical Contractors
National Association
401 Shatto Place
Los Angeles, CA 90020
213-487-7313

-847-

Electrical Contractors
Trust
4900 Hopyard Road
Pleasanton, CA 94566
925-833-7966

-848-

Electrical Training
Trust

515 Avenue 19
Los Angeles, CA 90031
323-221-5881
-849-
Electronic Document
Systems Association
24238 Hawthorne Blvd.
Torrance, CA 90505
310-373-3633 or 800-
669-7567
-850-
Electronic
Representatives
Association
P.O. Box 545
San Carlos, CA 94070
650-341-3596
-851-
Electronics Design
Automation Consortium
111 W. St. John Street
San Jose, CA 95113
408-287-3322
-852-
Employee Benefit
Planning Association
714 West Olympic Blvd.,
Ste. 710
Los Angeles, CA 90015
213-742-0756
-853-
Engineering and General
Contractors Association
P.O. Box 81798
San Diego, CA 92138
619-692-0760
-854-
Engineering and Utility
Contractors Association
7041 Koll Center
Parkway, Ste. 130
Pleasanton, CA 94566
925-846-9600
-855-
Engineering
Contractors'
Association
8310 Florence Avenue
Downey, Ca 90240
562-861-0929
-856-
Engineers and
Architects Association
350 S. Figueroa Street,
Ste. 600
Los Angeles, CA 90071
213-620-6920
-857-
Engineers' Council
P.O. Box 5012
Woodland Hills, CA
91403
818-992-8292
-858-
Escrow Institute of
California
1127 11th Street, Ste.
1003
Sacramento, CA 95814

916-442-1303
-859-
Evangelical Lutheran
Education Association
73 N. Hill Avenue
Pasadena, CA 91106
626-792-6027
-860-
Executives Association
of San Francisco
493 8th Avenue
San Francisco, CA 94118
415-221-5115
-861-
Faculty Association of
California Community
Colleges
926 J Street, Ste. 211
Sacramento, CA 95814
916-447-8555
-862-
Fashion Group
International of Los
Angeles
P.O. Box 6061-161
Sherman Oaks, CA 91423
818-990-0250
-863-
Family Winemakers of
California
1400 K Street
Sacramento, CA 95814
916-498-7500
-864-
Federation of Exchange
Accommodators
1127 11th Street
Sacramento, CA 95814
916-388-1031
-865-
Female Executives
Network
1588 Gilbreth Road
Burlingame, CA 94010
650-692-3836
-866-
Financial Executives
Institute
2975 Bowers Avenue
Santa Clara, CA 95051
408-567-9823
-867-
Financial Institutions
Insurance Association
21 Tamal Vista Blvd.,
Ste. 125
Corte Madera, CA 94925
415-924-8122
-868-
Financial Management
for Data Processing
P.O. Box 27543, 145 San
Benito Way
San Francisco, CA 94127
415-731-3706
-869-
Financial Women's
Association of San
Francisco

P.O. Box 26143
San Francisco, CA 94126
415-281-0861
-870-
Fire Districts
Association of
California
825 M Street
Rio Linda, CA 95673
916-991-7845
-871-
Fire Police Rescue
Medical Association
P.O. Box 94327
Pasadena, CA 91109
616-442-7043
-872-
Floor Covering
Institute
400 Reed Street
Santa Clara, CA 95060
408-727-2252
-873-
Food and Beverage
Association of San
Diego County
2515 Camino del Rio
South, Ste. 220
San Diego, CA 92108
619-298-1890
-874-
Foreign Trade
Association of Southern
California
900 Wilshire Blvd.,
Ste. 1434
Los Angeles, CA 90017
213-627-0634
-875-
Forest Landowners of
California
908 9th Street, 16th
Floor
Sacramento, CA 95814
916-972-0273
-876-
Forest Resources
Council
1115 11th Street, Ste.
100
Sacramento, CA 95814
916-448-2162
-877-
French American Chamber
of Commerce of San
Francisco
425 Bush Street, Ste.
401
San Francisco, CA 94108
415-398-2449
-878-
French-American Chamber
of Commerce
8222 Melrose Avenue
Los Angeles, CA 90046
323-651-4741
-879-
Fresh Produce and
Floral Council

6301 Beach Blvd., Ste,
150
Buena Park, CA 90621
714-739-0177
-880-
Garment Contractors
Association of Southern
California
110 East 9th Street,
Ste. A701
Los Angeles , CA 90079
213-629-4422
-881-
Geothermal Energy
Resources Council
P.O. Box 1350
Davis, CA 95617
530-758-2360
-882-
German American Chamber
of Commerce
465 California Street,
Ste. 506
San Francisco, CA 94104
415-392-2262
-883-
Golden Gate Business
Association (Gay and
Lesbian business
people)
584 Castro Street
San Francisco, CA 94114
415-441-3651
-884-
Golden Gate Ports
Association
303 World Trade Center
San Francisco, CA 94111
415-986-0693
-885-
Golden Gate Restaurant
Association
720 Market Street, Ste.
200
San Francisco, CA 94102
415-781-5348
-886-
Graphic Artists Guild,
Northern California
Chapter
P.O. Box 460946
San Francisco, CA 94146
415-995-4905
-887-
Greater Los Angeles
African American
Chamber of Commerce
3910 West Martin Luther
King Blvd.
Los Angeles, CA 90008
213-292-1297
-888-
Greater Los Angeles
Press Club
6255 Sunset Blvd., Ste.
2000
Hollywood, CA 90028
323-469-8180
-889-

Grocery Manufacturers
of America
915 L Street, Ste. 1110
Sacramento, CA 95814
916-447-9425
-890-
Health Officers
Association of
California
5050 Laguna Blvd., Ste.
112-580
Elk Grove, CA 95708
916-441-7405
-891-
The Healthcare Forum
425 Market Street, 16th
Floor
San Francisco, CA 94105
415-356-4300
-892-
Hispanic Business
Association, Anaheim
P.O. Box 2367
Anaheim, CA 92804
714-535-5899
-893-
Hispanic Chamber of
Commerce, Alameda
County
P.O. Box 1709
Oakland, CA 94606
510-536-4477
-894-
Hispanics in
Philanthropy
2606 Dwight Way
Berkeley, CA 94704
510-649-1690
-895-
Hollywood Radio and
Television Society
13701 Riverside Drive,
Ste. 205
Sherman Oaks, CA 91423
818-789-1182 -
-896-
Home Furnishings
Representatives Guild
of Southern California
1933 South Broadway,
Ste. 157
Los Angeles, CA 90007
213-747-1463
-897-
Home Warranty
Association of
California
17615 Kittridge Street
Van Nuys, CA 91406
818-881-1183
-898-
Hospitality Industry
Association
1355 Market Street, Ste
425C
San Francisco, CA 94103
415-861-5484
-899-

Hotel Council of San
Francisco
323 Geary Street, Ste.
517
San Francisco, CA 94102
415-391-5197
-900-
IDEA, The Health and
Fitness Source
(fitness professionals)
6190 Cornerstone Court
East, Ste. 204
San Diego, CA 92121
619-535-8979
-901-
Iceberg Lettuce
Advisory Board
512 Pajaro Street
Salinas, CA 93901
831-424-3782
-902-
Image Industry Council
International
P.O. Box 422643
San Francisco, CA 94142
415-905-5727
-903-
Independent Automobile
Dealers Association of
California
1900 Point West Way,
Ste. 144
Sacramento, CA 95815
916-924-5230
-904-
Independent Colleges of
Southern California
555 S. Flower Street,
Ste. 610
Los Angeles, CA 90071
213-553-9380
-905-
Independent Community
Bankers Association
500 Newport Center
Drive, Ste 960
Newport Beach, CA 92660
949-644-2606
-906-
Independent Energy
Producers Association
1112 I Street, Ste. 380
Sacramento, CA 95814
916-448-9499
-907-
Independent Insurance
Agents and Brokers of
the West
1000 Broadway, Ste. 600
Oakland, CA 94607
510-663-7800
-908-
Independent Maintenance
Contractors Association
1716 X Street
Sacramento, CA 95818
916-444-9801
-909-

Independent Oil
Producers' Agency
222 West 6th Street,
Ste. 10
San Pedro, CA 90731
310-519-7254
-910-
Independent Press
Association
500 Howard Street
San Francisco, CA 94105
415-443-4237
-911-
Independent Retailers,
Inc.
4766 Park Granada Blvd.
Calabasas, CA 91302
818-591-1680
-912-
Indoor Golf Association
of America
4747 Moreno Blvd., Ste.
355
San Diego, CA 92117
619-273-0373
-913-
Information
Technologies Credit
Union Association
P.O. Box 160
Del Mar, CA 92014
619-792-3883
-914-
Institute of Electrical
and Electronic
Engineers, Los Angeles
Council
1515 W. 150th Street
Gardena, CA 90247
310-715-6796
-915-
Institute of Food
Technologists
2140 Shattuck Avenue,
Ste. 1101
Berkeley, CA 94704
510-848-0582
-916-
Institute of Food
Technology
P.O. Box 3724
Orange, CA 92857
714-282-0919
-917-
Institute of
Governmental Advocates
(lobbyists)
PMB C414
915 L Street
Sacramento, CA 95814
916-442-3648
-918-
Institute of Heating
and Air Conditioning
Industries
452 W. Broadway
Glendale, CA 91204
818-551-1555
-919-

Institute of Management
Accountants
P.O. Box 370127
San Diego, CA 92137
619-281-7252
-920-
Institute of
Mathematical Statistics
3401 Investment Blvd.,
Ste. 7
Hayward, CA 94545
510-783-8141
-921-
Institute of Real
Estate Management
350 S. Figueroa Street
Los Angeles, CA 90071
213-633-1990
-922-
Institute of Scrap
Recycling Industries,
California Chapters
1760 E. Slauson
Los Angeles, CA 90058
323-587-2277
-923-
Institutional Analysts
Society
3539 Ocean View Blvd.
Glendale, CA 91208
818-957-1400
-924-
Insulation Contractors
Association
1911 F Street
Sacramento, CA 95814
916-444-2950
-925-
Insurance Agents and
Brokers Legislative
Council
915 L Street, Ste. 1110
Sacramento, CA 95814
800-772-8998
-926-
Insurance Agents and
Brokers of the West
1000 Broadway, Ste. 600
Oakland, CA 94607
510-663-7800
-927-
Insurance Brokers
Society of Southern
California
P.O. Box 3879
Torrance, CA 90510
310-212-6006
-928-
Interment Association
of California
(cemeteries)
1116 24th Street
Sacramento, CA 95816
916-441-4533
-929-
International
AgriCenter, Inc.
P.O. Box 1475
Tulare, CA 93275

559-688-1751
-930-
International
Association for
Administrative
Professionals
P.O. Box 17451
Irvine, CA 92623
714-647-1640
-931-
International
Association for
Financial Planning
1651 East 4th Street,
Ste. 244
Santa Ana, CA 92701
714-542-0024
-932-
International
Association of Art
Digital Professionals
4220 Fair Avenue, Ste.
103
North Hollywood, CA
91602
818-509-2959
-933-
International
Association of Audio-
Visual Communicators
9531 Jamacha Blvd.,
Ste. 263
Spring Valley, CA 91977
619-461-1600
-934-
International
Association of Business
Communicators
1 Hallidie Plaza, Ste.
600
San Francisco, CA 94102
415-544-4700
-935-
International
Association of Credit
Card Investigators
385 Bel Marin Keys
Blvd., Ste. H
Novato, CA 94949
415-884-6600
-936-
International
Association of Plumbing
and Mechanical
Officials
20001 Walnut Drive S.
Walnut, CA 91789
909-595-8449
-937-
International
Chiropractors
Association of
California
9700 Business Park
Drive, Ste. 406
Sacramento, CA 95827
916-362-8816
-938-

International
Conference of Building
Officials
5360 Workman Mill Road
Whittier, CA 90601
562-699-0541
-939-
International Council
of Shopping Centers
19800 MacArthur Blvd.
Irvine, CA 92612
949-224-3830
-940-
International
Documentary Association
1551 South Robertson
Blvd., Ste. 201
Los Angeles, CA 90035
310-284-8422
-941-
International Institute
for Lath and Plaster
3127 Los Feliz Blvd.,
Los Angeles, CA 90039
323-660-4411
-942-
International Institute
of Municipal Clerks
1212 North San Dimas
Canyon Road
San Dimas, CA 91773
909-592-4462
-943-
International Llama
Association, California
Chapter
25900 Fairview Avenue
Hayward, CA 94542
510-582-3393
-944-
International
Middleware Association
(computers)
19022 Brookhaven Drive
Saratoga, CA 95070
408-725-1711
-945-
International Motion
Picture and Lecturers
Association
1455 Royal Blvd.
Glendale, CA 91207
818-2471-2910
-946-
International
Professional Surrogates
Association
P.O. Box 4282
Torrance, CA 90510
323-469-4720
-947-
International Right-of-
Way Association
13650 Gramercy Place
Gardena, CA 90249
310-538-0233
-948-

International Society
for General Semantics
(language)
P.O. Box 728
Concord, CA 94522
925-798-0311
-949-
International Sports
Massage Federation
2156 Newport Blvd.
Costa Mesa, CA 92627
949-642-0735
-950-
International Stress
Management Association
U.S. International
University
San Diego, CA 92131
619-635-4698
-951-
International Trade
Council
465 California Street,
9th Floor
San Francisco, CA 94104
415-392-4511
-952-
International
Transactional Analysis
Association (clinical
psychology)
450 Pacific Avenue,
Ste. 250
San Francisco, CA 94133
415-989-5640
-953-
Japan Business
Association of Southern
California
3868 Carson Street,
Ste. 108
Torrance, CA 90503
310-543-4606
-954-
Japanese Chamber of
Commerce of Northern
California
300 Montgomery Street,
Ste. 725
San Francisco, CA 94194
415-395-9353
-955-
Japanese Chamber of
Commerce of Southern
California
244 South San Pedro
Street, Ste. 504
Los Angeles, CA 90012
213-626-3067
-956-
Jungian Analysts
Society of San
Francisco (clinical
psychology)
2040 Gough Street
San Francisco, CA 94109
415-771-8055
-957-

Kiwifruit
Administrative
Committee
1540 River Park Drive,
Ste. 110
Sacramento, CA 95815
916-929-5314
-958-
Kiwifruit Marketing
Association of
California
730 Howe Avenue
Sacramento, CA 95825
916-645-8835
-959-
Korean American Grocers
Association of
California
4201 Wilshire Blvd.,
Ste. 623
los Angeles, CA 90010
323-937-3777
-960-
Korean American Women
Artists and Writers
Association
1426 Fillmore Street
San Francisco, CA 94115
415-567-1222
-961-
Korean Business Men's
Federation in America
3807 Wilshire Blvd.,
Ste. 400
Los Angeles, CA 90010
213-480-0757
-962-
Korean Caligraphers
Association U.S.A.
981 S. Western Avenue
Los Angeles, CA 90006
323-734-5432
-963-
Korean Chamber of
Commerce of Southern
California
3440 Wilshire Blvd.,
Ste. 520
Los Angeles, CA 90010
213-480-1115
-964-
Korean Dry Cleaners and
Laundry Association
14909 Crenshaw Blvd.,
Ste. 204
Gardena, CA 90249
310-679-1300
-965-
Korean Investors and
Traders Association
4801 Wilshire Blvd.
Los Angeles, CA 90010
323-939-9500
-966-
Latin American Dental
Association
528 Amalia Street
Los Angeles, CA 90022
323-262-2727

-967-
Latin Business
Association
5400 East Olympic
Blvd., Ste. 130
Los Angeles, CA 90022
323-721-4000
-968-
Lawn and Garden
Equipment Dealers
Coalition
18935 Van Buren Blvd.
Riverside, CA 92508
909-780-1788
-969-
Leading Jewelers Guild
2050 South Bundy Drive,
Ste. 210
Los Angeles, CA 90025
310-820-3386
-970-
Life Underwriters
Association of Los
Angeles
714 West Olympic Blvd.,
Ste. 710
Los Angeles, CA 90015
213-742-0756
-971-
Los Angeles Academy of
Medicine
5820 Wilshire Blvd.,
Ste. 500
Los Angeles, CA 90036
323-937-5514
-972-
Los Angeles Association
of Life Underwriters
P.O. Box 261084
Encino, CA 91426
818-784-8024
-973-
Los Angeles Business
Council
10850 Wilshire Blvd.
Los Angeles, CA 90024
310-475-4574
-974-
Los Angeles Business
Travel Association
1804 W. Burbank Blvd.
Burbank, CA 91506
310-544-2484
-975-
Los Angeles County Bar
Association (lawyers)
261 S. Figueroa Street,
3rd Fl.
Los Angeles, CA 90012
213-627-2727
-976-
Los Angeles County
Medical Association
523 W. 6th Street, 10th
Fl.
Los Angeles, CA 90051
213-683-9900
-977-

Los Angeles County
Professional Peace
Officers Association
1100 Corporate Center
Drive, Ste. 201
Monterey Park, CA 91754
323-261-3010
-978-
Los Angeles General
Agents and Managers
Association
714 West Olympic Blvd.,
Ste. 710
Los Angeles, CA 90015
213-742-0756
-979-
Los Angeles Music
Network
5757 Wilshire Blvd.,
Ste. 440
Los Angeles, CA 90036
323-904-4600
-980-
Los Angeles Retired
Fire and Police
Association
7521 Las Tunas Drive,
Ste. 4
Temple City, CA 91780
323-283-4441
-981-
Los Angeles Society of
Financial Analysts
900 Wilshire Blvd.,
Ste. 1434
Los Angeles, CA 90017
213-627-1500
-982-
Los Angeles Surgical
Society
5820 Wilshire Blvd.,
Ste. 500
Los Angeles, CA 90036
323-937-5514
-983-
Los Angeles-Ventura
Sales and Marketing
Council
24005 Ventura Blvd.
Calabasas, CA 91302
818-224-4516
-984-
Lumber Association of
California and Nevada
3130 Fite Circle
Sacramento, CA 95827
916-369-7501
-985-
Magazine
Representatives
Association
6404 Wilshire Blvd.,
Ste. 1111
Los Angeles, CA 90048
323-655-1951
-986-
Manufacturers' Agents
National Association
P.O. Box 3467

Laguna Hills, CA 92654
949-859-4040
-987-
Manufacturers'
Disposable Medical
Supplies Coalition
725 30th Street, Ste.
102
Sacramento, CA 95816
916-447-9999
-988-
Marina and Recreation
Association
915 L Street, Ste. C
Sacramento, CA 95814
916-441-1475
-989-
Marine Corps Aviation
Association
7000 Trabuco Road
Irvine, CA 92718
949-857-6437
-990-
Marine Corps Drill
Instructors Association
4085 Pacific Highway
San Diego, CA 92110
619-688-0864
-991-
Marketing Association
of California
74 New Montgomery
Street
San Francisco, CA 94105
415-764-4826
-992-
Marshals Association
14455 Civic Drive
Victorville, CA 92392
760-243-8756
-993-
Mason Contractors
Exchange of Southern
California
2550 Beverly Blvd.
Los Angeles, CA 90057
213-388-0476
-994-
Masonry Institute of
America
2550 Beverly Blvd.
Los Angeles, CA 90057
213-388-0472 or 800-
221-4000
-995-
Media Alliance
814 Mision Street, Ste.
205
San Francisco, CA 94103
415-546-6334
-996-
Medical Marketing
Association
74 New Montgomery
Street, Ste. 230
San Francisco, CA 94105
415-764-4807
-997-

Meeting Planners
International,
Sacramento
530 Bercut Drive, Ste.
G
Sacramento, CA 95814
916-443-0363
-998-
Meeting Planners
International, Southern
California Chapter
5855 Green Valley
Circle
Culver City, CA 90230
310-216-9674
-999-
Merchants and
Manufacturers
Association
1150 South Olive
Street, Ste. 2300
Los Angeles, CA 90015
213-748-0421
-1000-
Mexican American
Grocers Association
405 North San Fernando
Road
Los Angeles, CA 90031
323-227-1565
-1001-
Milk Producers Council
13545 Euclid Avenue
Ontario, CA 91761
909-628-6018
-1002-
Mosquito and Vector
Control Association of
California
8633 Bond Road
Elk Grove, CA 95624
916-685-2600
-1003-
Motion Picture and
Television Credit
Association
4102 W. Magnolia Blvd.,
Ste. A
Burbank, CA 91505
818-729-0220
-1004-
Motion Picture and
Television Fund
23388 Mulholland Drive
Woodland Hills, CA
91364
818-876-1145
-1005-
Motion Picture Export
Association of America
15503 Ventura Blvd.
Encino, CA 91436
818-995-6600
-1006-
Motorcycle Funeral
Escort Association of
California
2943 West Capitol
Avenue

West Sacramento, CA
95691
916-372-4406
-1007-
Motorcycle Industry
Council
2 Jenner Street, Ste.
150
Irvine, CA 92718
949-727-4211
-1008-
Motorcycle Safety
Foundation
2 Jenner Street, Ste.
150
Irvine, CA 92718
949-727-3227
-1009-
Multilevel Marketing
International
Association
1101 Dove Street, Ste.
170
Newport Beach, CA 92660
949-854-0484
-1010-
Mushroom Council
2200-B Douglas Blvd.,
Ste. 220
Roseville, CA 95661
916-781-7585
-1011-
Napa Valley Wine
Growers Alliance
P.O. Box 106
Oakville, CA 94562
707-226-1395
-1012-
National Academy of
Document Examiners
920 S. Robertson Blvd.
Los Angeles, CA 90035
310-652-9978
-1013-
National Academy of
Recording Arts and
Sciences
3402 Pico Blvd.
Santa Monica, CA 90405
310-392-3777
-1014-
National Academy of
Television Arts and
Sciences
P.O. Box 80255
San Diego, CA 92138
619-297-1388
-1015-
National Agricultural
Marketing Association
9710 Scranton Road,
Ste. 110
San Diego, CA 92121
619-453-3761
-1016-
National Association
for Physical Education
in Higher Education

c/o Department of Human
Performance, San Jose
State University, Attn:
Dr. Gail Evans
San Jose, CA 95192
408-924-3029
-1017-
National Association of
Black Accountants
P.O. Box 71175
Los Angeles, CA 90071
323-665-2682
-1018-
National Association of
Business Travel Agents
3699 Wilshire Blvd.,
Ste. 7000
Los Angeles, CA 90010
213-382-3335
-1019-
National Association of
Composers
P.O. Box 49256,
Barrington Station
Los Angeles, CA 90049
310-541-8213
-1020-
National Association of
Computer Consultant
Businesses, Northern
California
32 Moody Court
San Rafael, CA 94901
415-485-1439
-1021-
National Association of
Credit Union Chairmen
P.O. Box 160
Del Mar, CA 92014
619-792-3883
-1022-
National Association of
Free Agents
P.O. Box 189040
Sacramento, CA 95818
916-442-2476
-1023-
National Association of
Gas Chlorinators
30575 Trabuco Canyon
Road, Ste. 105
Trabuco Canyon, CA
92679
949-459-8735
-1024-
National Association of
Independent Fee
Appraisers
1127 11th Street, Ste.
242
Sacramento, CA 95814
916-448-3381
-1025-
National Association of
Independent Insurers
980 9th Street, 16th
Floor
Sacramento, CA 95814
916-446-2009

-1026-
National Association of
Industrial Office Parks
1250 6th Avenue
San Diego, CA 92101
619-231-8511
-1027-
National Association of
Manufacturers
703 Market Street, Ste.
1510
San Francisco, CA 94103
415-243-9115
-1028-
National Association of
Music Merchants
5790 Armada Drive
Carlsbad, CA 92008
760-438-8001
-1029-
National Association of
Pretrial Services
Agencies
P.O. Box 280808
San Francisco, CA 94128
650-588-0212
-1030-
National Association of
Railroad Trial Counsel
881 Alma Real Drive,
Ste. 218
Pacific Palisades, CA
90272
310-459-7659
-1031-
National Association of
Securities Dealers
525 Market Street, Ste.
300
San Francisco, CA 94105
415-882-1200
-1032-
National Association of
Seventh Day Adventist
Dentists
P.O. Box 101
Loma Linda, CA 92354
909-794-8025
-1033-
National Association of
Social Workers,
California Chapter
1016 23rd Street
Sacramento, CA 95816
916-442-4565
-1034-
National Association of
Social Workers,
California Chapter
6030 Wilshire Blvd.,
Ste. 202
Los Angeles, CA 90036
323-935-2050
-1035-
National Association of
Television Program
Executives
2425 Olympic Blvd.,
Ste. 550-E

Santa Monica, CA 90404
310-453-4440
-1036-
National Association of
Theatre Owners
4605 Lankershim Blvd.,
Ste. 340
North Hollywood, CA
91602
818-506-1778
-1037-
National Association of
the Remodeling Industry
P.O. Box 110400
Campbell, CA 95011
408-559-4996
-1039-
National Association of
Women Business Owners
550 Carson Plaza Drive,
Ste. 127
Carson, CA 90746
310-352-4974
-1040-
National Association of
Women Business Owners
780 Montague
Expressway, Ste. 204
San Jose, CA 95131
408-257-3857
-1041-
National Association of
Women in Construction
P.O. Box 880725
San Diego, CA 92188
619-455-9205
-1042-
National Association on
Crime and Delinquency
685 Market Street, Ste.
620
San Francisco, CA 94105
415-896-6223
-1043-
National Automatic
Merchandising
Association
16030 Ventura Blvd.
Encino, CA 91436
818-783-8363
-1044-
National Bicycle
Dealers Association
777 W. 19th Street,
Suite O
Costa Mesa, CA 92627
949-722-6909
-1045-
National Black Public
Relations Society
6565 Sunset Blvd. Ste.,
301
Hollywood, CA 90028
323-466-8221
-1046-
National Bureau of
Certified Consultants
Management Consulting
Center

3577 4th Avenue
San Diego, CA 92103
619-297-2207
-1047-
National Casino
Executives Association
1730 I Street, Ste. 240
Sacramento, CA 95814
916-443-9023
-1048-
National Coalition of
Independent Scholars
P.O. Box 5743
Berkeley, CA 94705
510-540-8415
-1049-
National Council of
Postal Credit Unions
P.O. Box 160
Del Mar, CA 92014
619-792-3883
-1050-
National Education
Association
1350 Bayshore Highway
Burlingame, CA 94010
650-347-6000
-1051-
National Electrical
Contractors Association
3960 Industrial Blvd.,
Ste. 200B
Sacramento, CA 95891
916-376-8980
-1052-
National Electrical
Contractors Association
401 Shatto Place
Los Angeles, CA 90020
213-487-7313
-1053-
National Electrical
Contractors Association
P.O. Box 3639
San Diego, CA 92186
619-298-1183
-1054-
National Electrical
Contractors Association
1493 Park Avenue
San Jose, CA 95126
408-288-6100
-1055-
National Employment
Lawyers Association
600 Harrison Street,
Ste. 535
San Francisco, CA 94107
415-227-4655
-1056-
National Exchange
Carrier Association
1320 Willow Pass Road,
Ste. 550
Concord, CA 94520
925-687-0401
-1057-
National Farmers
Organization

2853 Geer Road, Ste. C
Turlock, CA 95382
209-634-6455
-1058-
National Federation of
Independent Business
455 Capitol Mall, Ste.
225
Sacramento, CA 95814
916-448-9904
-1059-
National Federation of
Information Consultants
P.O. Box 189040
Sacramento, CA 95818
-1060-
National Flute
Association
P.O. Box 800597
Santa Clarita, CA 91380
805-297-5287
-1061-
National Guard
Association of
California
1117 2nd Street
Sacramento, CA 95814
916-448-6725
-1062-
National Lawyers Guild
558 Capp Street
San Francisco, CA 94110
415-285-5067
-1063-
National Management
Association
523 Cityscape Place
San Jose, CA 95136
408-264-1295
-1064-
National Marine
Educators
P.O. Box 51215
Pacific Grove, CA 93950
408-648-4837
-1065-
National Meat
Association
1970 Broadway, Ste. 825
Oakland, CA 94612
510-763-1533
-1066-
National Nutritional
Food Association
3931 MacArthur Blvd.,
Ste. 101
Newport Beach, CA 92660
949-622-6272
-1067-
National Organization
of Test, Research and
Training Reactors
SM-ALC/LI-5
5335 Price Avenue,
McClellan AFB
Sacramento, CA 95652
916-643-1024
-1068-

National Retired
Teachers Association
3200 E. Carson Street
Lakewood, CA 90712
562-496-2277
-1069-
National School Boards
Association
400 Capitol Mall
Sacramento, CA 95814
916-449-3929
-1070-
National Society of
Fundraising Executives
1644 Linbrook Drive
San Diego, CA 92111
619-277-9076
-1071-
National Society of
Real Estate Appraisers
1127 11th Street, Ste.
242
Sacramento, CA 95814
916-448-3381
-1072-
National Store Fixture
and Display Association
c/o Daniel's Display
1267 Mission Street
San Francisco, CA 94103
415-861-4400
-1073-
National Vehicle
Leasing Association
800 Airport Blvd.
Burlingame, CA 94010
650-548-9135
-1074-
Nationwide Truckers
Association
2940 E. La Palma Avenue
Anaheim, CA 92806
714-961-8096
-1075-
Natural Colored Wool
Growers Association
P.O. Box 487
Willits, CA 95490
707-459-8094
-1076-
New Car Dealers
Association of San
Diego County
10065 Mesa Ridge Court
San Diego, CA 92121
619-550-0080
-1077-
Nisei Farmers League
(Japanese-American
farmers labor
relations)
5108 East Clinton Way,
Ste. 115
Fresno, CA 93727
559-251-8468
-1078-
North American Council
of Automotive Teachers

11956 Bernardo Plaza
Drive, PMB 436
San Diego, CA 92128
619-487-8126
-1079-
Northern California
Asphalt Producers
Association
P.O. Box 2201
Nevada City, CA 95959
530-478-9321
-1080-
Northern California
Council of Black
Professional Engineers
2708 Ritchie Street
Oakland, CA 94605
510-632-9736
-1081-
Northern California
Direct Marketing Club
500 Sutter Street, Ste.
906
San Francisco, CA 94102
415-434-1696
-1082-
Northern California
Golf Association
P.O. Box NCGA
Pebble Beach, CA 93953
831-625-4653
-1083-
Northern California
Grantmakers
(philanthropy)
116 New Montgomery
Street, Ste. 742
San Francisco, CA 94105
415-777-5761
-1084-
Northern California
Grocers Association
1807 Tribute Road
Sacramento, CA 95815
916-929-9741
-1085-
Northern California
Human Resources Council
360 Pine Street
San Francisco, CA 94104
415-291-1992
-1086-
Northern California
Marine Association
30 Jack London Square,
Ste. 204
Oakland, CA 94607
510-834-1000
-1087-
Northern California Ob-
Gyn Society
(obstectrics and
gynaecology)
P.O. Box 160162
Sacramento, CA 95816
916-558-0150
-1088-

Northern California Professional Golfers Association
2133 A Las Positas Court, Ste. A
Livermore, CA 94550
925-455-7800
-1089-

Northern California Psychiatric Society
1631 Ocean Avenue
San Francisco, CA 94112
415-334-2418
-1090-

Northern California Society of Association Executives
74 New Montgomery Street, Ste. 230
San Francisco, CA 94105
415-764-4942
-1091-

Northern California Society of Oral and Maxillofacial Surgeons
151 N. Sunrise Avenue, Ste. 1304
Roseville, CA 95661
916-772-9221
-1092-

Northern California Solar Energy Association
P.O. Box 3008
Berkeley, CA 94703
510-869-2759
-1093-

Northern California Tavern and Restaurant Association
323 Geary Street
San Francisco, CA 94102
415-986-2872
-1094-

Northern California Water Association
455 Capitol Mall, Ste. 335
Sacramento, CA 95814
916-442-8333
-1095-

Oakland World Trade Association
530 Water Street, 7th Fl.
Oakland, CA 94607
Requested phone not be listed
-1096-

Obstetrical and Gynecological Assembly of Southern California
5820 Wilshire Blvd., Ste. 500
Los Angeles, CA 90036
323-937-5514
-1097-

Occupational Therapy Association of California
4600 Northgate Blvd., Ste. 135
Sacramento, CA 95834
916-567-7000
-1098-

Officers for Justice (association of peace officers)
5126 3rd Street
San Francisco, CA 94124
415-822-2225
-1099-

Olive Growers Council
121 East Main Street, Ste. 4
Visalia, CA 93291
559-734-1710
-1100-

Ophthalmic Photographers Society
California Pacific Medical Center, Eye Professional Services
2100 Webster Street, Ste. 219
San Francisco, CA 94115
415-923-3937
-1101-

Organization of News Ombudsmen
c/o Sacramento Bee
P.O. Box 15779
Sacramento, CA 95852
916-442-8050
-1102-

Organization of Professional Acting Coaches and Teachers
3968 Eureka Drive
Studio City, CA 91604
323-877-4988
-1103-

Osteopathic Physicians and Surgeons of California
1900 Point West Way, Ste. 188
Sacramento, CA 95815
916-561-0724
-1104-

Outpatient Ophthamalic Surgery Society
P.O. Box 23220
San Diego, CA 92193
619-692-4426
-1105-

Oxygen Society
74 New Montgomery Street
San Francisco, CA 94105
415-546-3124
-1106-

Pacific Association of Building Service Contractors
3550 Foothill Blvd.

Glendale, CA 91214
818-247-8778
-1107-

Pacific Coast Builders Conference
1215 K Street, Ste. 1200
Sacramento, CA 95814
916-325-9300
-1108-

Pacific Coast Coffee Association
101 The Embarcadero
San Francisco, CA 94105
415-986-0267
-1109-

Pacific Coast Federation of Fishermen's Associations
Old Coast Guard Building
The Presidio
P.O. Box 29910
San Francisco, CA 94129
415-561-5080
-1110-

Pacific Coast Gas Association
1350 Bayshore Highway, Ste. 440
Burlingame, CA 94010
650-579-7000
-1111-

Pacific Coast Quarter Horse Association
560 Wall Street, Ste. A
Auburn, CA 95603
530-823-5991
-1112-

Pacific Coast Renderers Association
1521 I Street
Sacramento, CA 95814
916-441-2272
-1113-

Pacific Coast Society of Orthodontists
1323 Columbus Avenue, Ste. 301
San Francisco, CA 94133
415-441-2410
-1114-

Pacific Economy and Trade Association
690 Market Street
San Francisco, CA 94104
415-956-6560
-1114-

Pacific Egg and Poultry Association
1521 I Street
Sacramento, CA 95814
916-441-0801
-1115-

Pacific Merchant Shipping Association

550 California Street,
Sacramento Street Tower
no. 113
San Francisco, CA 94104
415-352-0710
-1116-
Pacific Pioneer
Broadcasters
P.O. Box 4866
North Hollywood, CA
91607
323-461-2121
-1117
Pacific Water Quality
Association
2124 Main Street, Ste.
110
Huntington Beach, CA
92648
714-960-2428
-1118-
Painting and Decorating
Contractors Association
of San Diego County
4168 Poplar Street,
Ste. A
San Diego, CA 92105
619-280-7322
-1119-
Painting and Decorating
Contractors of
California
3504 Walnut Avenue,
Ste. A
Carmichael, CA 95608
916-972-1055
-1120-
Parking Association of
California
14156 Magnolia Blvd.
Sherman Oaks, CA 91423
818-986-0533
-1121-
Peace Officers Research
Association of
California
2495 Natomas Park
Drive, Ste. 555
Sacramento, CA 95833
916-921-0660
-1122-
PEN Center USA West
(writers and others in
the literary community)
672 S. Lafayette Park
Place, Ste. 41
Los Angeles, CA 90057
213-365-8500
-1123-
Personal Insurance
Federation of
California
980 9th Street, Ste.
2030
Sacramento, CA 95814
916-442-6646
-1124-
Pest Control Operators
of California

3031 Beacon Blvd.
West Sacramento, CA
95691
916-372-4363
-1125-
Plastering Contractors
Association
2402 Vista Nobleza
Newport Beach, CA 92660
949-640-9903
-1126-
Plumbing and Piping
Industry Council
370 Amapola Avenue,
Ste. 203
Torrance, CA 90501
310-381-3040
-1127-
Plumbing-Heating-
Cooling Contractors of
California
1911 F Street
Sacramento, CA 95814
916-446-7422
-1128-
Power Sources
Manufacturers
Association
3685 Motor Avenue, Ste.
240
Los Angeles, CA 90034
310-287-1826
-1129-
Press Club of San
Francisco
155 Sansome Street
San Francisco, CA 94104
415-986-7800
-1130-
Printing Industries
Association of San
Diego
3914 Murphy Canyon
Road, Ste. A107
San Diego, CA 92123
619-571-6555
-1131-
Printing Industries of
Northern California
665 3rd Street, Ste.
500
San Francisco, CA 94107
916-485-0504
-1132-
Printing Industries of
Southern California
5800 S. Eastern Avenue
Los Angeles, CA 90040
323-808-9990
-1133-
Processing Strawberry
Advisory Board
P.O. Box 929
Watsonville, CA 95077
408-724-5454
-1134-
Producers Guild of
America

400 South Beverly
Drive, Ste. 211
Beverly Hills, CA 90212
310-557-0807
-1135-
Producers Livestock
Marketing Association
P.O. Box 510
Madera, CA 93639
209-674-4674
-1136-
Professional and
Technical Consultants
Association
P.O. Box 4143
Mountain View, CA 94040
650-903-8305
-1137-
Professional
Association for
Childhood Education
74 New Montgomery
Street, Ste. 230
San Francisco, CA 94105
415-764-4805
-1138-
Professional
Association of
Specialty Contractors
4345 Murphy Canyon Road
San Diego, CA 92123
619-503-1563
-1139-
Professional Educators
of Los Angeles
22543 Ventura Blvd.,
Ste. 218
Woodland Hills, CA
91364
818-225-1343
-1140-
Professional Engineers
in California
Government
660 J Street, Ste. 445
Sacramento, CA 95814
916-446-0400
-1141-
Professional Fiduciary
Association of
California
P.O. Box 661813
Sacramento, CA 95866
916-927-8836
-1142-
Professional Golfers'
Association
601 South Valencia
Avenue, Ste. 200
Brea, CA 92621
714-776-4653
-1143-
Professional Insurance
Agents of California
and Nevada
1315 I Street, Ste. 200
Sacramento, CA 95814
916-443-4221
-1144-

Professional
Numismatics Guild
3950 Concordia Lane
Fallbrook, CA 92028
760-728-1300
-1145-
Professionals in Human
Resources Association
888 S. Figueroa Street,
Ste. 1050
Los Angeles, CA 90017
213-622-7472
-1146-
Promotional Marketing
Association
3031 F Street
Sacramento, CA 95816
916-443-4453
-1147-
Prune Bargaining
Association
335 Teagarden Avenue,
Ste. B
Yuba City, CA 95991
530-674-5636
-1148-
Public Health
Laboratory Association
of California
505 South Beverly
Drive, Box 1119
Beverly Hills, CA 90212
-1149-
Public Links Golf
Association of Southern
California
7035 East Orangethorpe
Avenue, Ste. E
Buena Park, CA 90621
714-994-4747
-1150-
Publishers Marketing
Association
627 S. Aviation Way
Manhattan Beach, CA
90266
310-372-2732
-1151-
Purchasing Management
Association of Los
Angeles
2100 N. Sepulveda
Street
Manhattan Beach, CA
90266
310-545-2882
-1152-
Purchasing Management
Association of Northern
California
P. O. Box 12156
San Francisco, CA 94112
415-585-6018
-1153-
Radio and Television
News Association
15030 Ventura Blvd.,
Ste. 742
Sherman oaks, CA 91403

818-986-8168
-1154-
Raisin Administrative
Committee
P.O. Box 5217
Fresno, CA 93755
559-225-0520
-1155-
Raisin Bargaining
Association
3425 North First
Street, Ste. 209
Fresno, CA 93726
559-221-1925
-1156-
Realty Investment
Association of
California
17802 Irvine Blvd.
Tustin, CA 92780
714-554-6604
-1157-
Recreation Vehicle
Industry Association
1748 West Katella, Ste.
108
Orange, CA 92867
213-485-0254
-1158-
Regional Credit
Association
P.O. Box 1390
Rancho Cordova, CA
95741
916-638-1113
-1159-
Religious Speech
Communication
Association
Azusa Pacific
University
Azusa, CA 91702
626-815-6000, ext. 3489
-1160-
Rental Industry
Association
216 North E Street
Woodland, CA 95695
530-666-4337
-1161-
Residential Drywall
Association
2402 Vista Nobleza
Newport Beach, CA 92660
949-640-9902
-1162-
Retired Public
Employees Association
300 T Street
Sacramento, CA 95814
916-441-7732
-1163-
Rice Growers
Association of
California
P.O. Box 958
Sacramento, CA 95812
916-371-6941
-1164-

Roofing Contractors
Association of
California
2215 21st Street
Sacramento, CA 95818
916-456-4790
-1165-
Roundtable for Women
and Food Services
816 E. 4th Avenue
San Mateo, CA 94401
650-344-1642
-1166-
Sales and Marketing
Council
24005 Ventura Blvd.
Calabasas, CA
818-224-4516
-1167-
Sales and Marketing
Executives of the Bay
Area
417 Montgomery Street,
Ste. 410
San Francisco, CA 94104
415-693-9515
-1168-
San Diego Association
of Life Underwriters
2515 Camino del Rio
South, Ste. 242A
San Diego, CA 92108
619-298-1243
-1169-
San Diego Association
of Mortgage Brokers
5060 Shoreham Place
San Diego, CA 92122
619-450-6566
-1170-
San Diego Black Nurses
Association
P.O. Box 740088
San Diego 92174
619-262-9133
-1171-
San Diego Black Police
Officers Association
101 50th Street
San Diego, CA 92102
619-262-8800
-1172-
San Diego Computer
Society
5694 Mission Center
Road, Ste. 602, Box 350
San Diego, CA 92138
619-549-3787
-1173-
San Diego County
Apartment Association
2727 Camino del Rio
South, Ste. 327
San Diego, CA 92108
619-297-1000
-1174-
San Diego County Bar
Association (lawyers)
1333 7th Avenue

San Diego, CA 92101
619-231-0781
-1175-
San Diego County Rock
Products Association
2831 Camino del Rio
South, Ste. 203
San Diego, CA 92108
619-260-8316
-1176-
San Diego County
Veterinary Medical
Association
462 Alvarado Canyon
Road
San Diego, CA 92120
619-640-9583
-1177-
San Diego Direct
Marketing Association
6603 Convoy Court
San Diego, CA 92111
619-503-1471
-1178-
San Diego Education
Association
10393 San Diego Mission
Road, Ste. 100
San Diego, CA 92108
619-283-4411
-1179-
San Diego Legal
Secretaries Association
3333 Camino del Rio
South, Ste. 340
San Diego, CA 92108
619-233-5729
-1180-
San Diego Lumber
Association
P.O. Box 82868
San Diego, CA 92138
619-232-6163
-1181-
San Diego Press Club
2454 Heritage Park Row
San Diego, CA 92110
619-299-5747
-1182-
San Diego Psychological
Association
2535 Camino del Rio
South, Ste. 220
San Diego, CA 92108
619-297-4825
-1183-
San Diego Restaurant
Association
1620 5th Avenue, Ste.
940
San Diego, CA 92106
619-230-0764
-1184-
San Diego Roofing
Contractors Association
3288 El Cajon Blvd.,
Ste. 4
San Diego, CA 92104
619-283-1225

-1185-
San Francisco
Advertising Club
150 Post Street, Ste.
325
San Francisco, CA 94108
415-986-3878
-1186-
San Francisco Apartment
Association
333 Hayes Street, Ste.
100
San Francisco, CA 94102
415-255-2288
-1187-
San Francisco
Association of Legal
Assistants
P.O. Box 2110
San Francisco, CA 94126
415-777-2390
-1188-
San Francisco Dental
Society
2143 Lombard Street
San Francisco, CA 94123
415-928-7337
-1189-
San Francisco
Electrical Contractors
Association
555 Gough Street
San Francisco, CA 94102
415-703-8333
-1190-
San Francisco Fashion
Industries
1000 Brannan Street
San Francisco, CA 94103
415-621-6100
-1191-
San Francisco Hispanic
Chamber of Commerce
2601 Mission Street,
Ste. 900
San Francisco, CA 94110
415-647-0224
-1192-
San Francisco Hotel
Association
323 Geary Street, Ste.
611
San Francisco, CA 94102
415-392-7860
-1193-
San Francisco Police
Officers Association
510 7th Street
San Francisco, CA 94103
415-861-5060
-1194-
San Francisco Produce
Association
2095 Jerrold Avenue,
Ste. 212
San Francisco, CA 94124
415-550-4495
-1195-

San Francisco
Professional Food
Society
816 E. 4th Avenue
San Mateo, CA 94401
650-344-1642
-1196-
San Francisco
Restaurant Association
720 Market Street, Ste.
200
San Francisco, CA 94102
415-781-5348
-1197-
San Francisco Trial
Lawyers Association
World Trade Center,
Ste. 207
San Francisco, CA 94111
415-956-6401
-1198-
San Joaquin Valley Hay
Growers Association
P.O. Box 1127
Tracy, CA 95378
209-835-1662
-1199-
Scaffold Industry
Association
20335 Ventura Blvd.,
Ste. 310
Woodland Hills, CA
91364
818-610-0320
-1200-
School Facility
Manufacturers'
Association
1130 K Street, Ste. 210
Sacramento, CA 95814
916-441-3300
-1201-
Screen Actors Guild
5757 Wilshire Blvd.
Los Angeles, CA 90036
323-954-1600
-1202-
Security Analysts of
San Francisco
San Francisco Bay Area
650-994-2565
-1203-
Seismological Society
of America
201 Plaza Professional
Building
El Cerrito, CA 94530
510-525-5474
-1204-
Semiconductor Equipment
and Materials
International
805 East Middlefield
Road
Mountain View, CA 94043
650-964-5111
-1205-
Semiconductor Industry
Association

181 Metro Drive, Ste. 450
San Jose, CA 95110
408-436-6600
-1206-
Sheet Metal and Air Conditioning Contractors National Association
9951 Horn Road
Sacramento, CA 95827
916-366-1688
-1207-
Sheet Metal and Air Conditioning Contractors National Association
1450 E. 17th Street
Santa Ana, CA 92705
714-547-1821
-1208-
Sheet Metal Industry Fund of Los Angeles
12070 Telegraph Road, Ste. 350
Santa Fe Springs, CA 90670
562-944-6345
-1209-
Silicon Valley Manufacturing Group
226 Airport Parkway
San Jose, CA 95110
408-501-7864
-1210-
Singapore American Business Association
2 Challen Court
Alameda, CA 94501
510-252-1160
-1211-
Small Business of America
P.O. Box 1629
Gilroy, CA 95021
408-848-2049
-1212-
Small School Districts' Association
1130 K Street, Ste. 216
Sacramento, CA 95814
916-444-9335
-1213-
Society for California Archaeology
c/o Department of Archaeology, California State University
Fullerton, CA 92634
-1214-
Society for Computer Simulation
P.O. Box 17900
San Diego, CA 92177
619-277-3888
-1215-
Society for History Education

California State University, Long Beach
1250 Bellflower Blvd.
Long Beach, CA 90840
562-985-1653
-1216-
Society for Human Resource Management
P.O. Box 19311
San Diego, CA 92159
619-589-0111
-1217-
Society for Information Display
31 E. Julian Street
San Jose, CA 95112
408-977-1013
-1218-
Society for Marketing Professional Services
2550 Beverly Blvd.
Los Angeles, CA 90057
213-388-0478
-1219-
Society for Orthomolecular Health Medicine
2698 Pacific Avenue
San Francisco, CA 94115
415-922-6462
-1220-
Society for the Advancement of Material and Process Engineering
P.O. Box 2459
Covina, CA 91722
626-331-0616
-1221-
Society of California Accountants
2131 Capitol Avenue, Ste. 101
Sacramento, CA 95816
916-443-2057
-1222-
Society of California Archivists
c/o ASUC Store, Box 605, Bancroft Way and Telegraph Avenue
Berkeley, CA 94720
-1223-
Society of Collision Repair Specialists
131 North Tustin Avenue, Ste. 210
Tustin, CA 92680
714-835-3110
-1224-
Society of Critical Care Medicine
8101 East Kaiser Blvd.
Anaheim, CA 92808
714-282-6000
-1225-
Society of Experimental Test Pilots
P.O. Box 986
Lancaster, CA 93584

805-942-9574
-1226-
Society of Financial Services, Los Angeles Chapter
714 West Olympic Blvd., Ste. 710
Los Angeles, CA 90015
213-742-0756
-1227-
Society of Graduate Surgeons
5820 Wilshire Blvd., Ste. 500
Los Angeles, CA 90036
323-937-5514
-1228-
Society of Hispanic Professional Engineers
5400 East Olympic Blvd., Ste. 210
Los Angeles, CA 90022
323-725-3970
-1229-
Society of Iranian Professionals
1659 Scott Blvd.
Santa Clara, CA 95050
408-261-0777
-1230-
Society of Magnetic Resonance
2118 Milvia Street, Ste. 201
Berkeley, CA 94704
510-841-1899
-1231-
Society of Motion Picture and Television Art Directors
11365 Ventura Blvd., Ste. 315
Studio City, CA 91604
818-762-9995
-1232-
Society of Singers
8242 W. Third Street, Ste. 250
Los Angeles, CA 90048
323-651-1696
-1233-
Society of Telecommunications Consultants
13766 Center Street, Ste. 212
Carmel Valley, CA 93924
831-659-0110
-1234-
Software Council of Southern California
21041 S. Western Avenue
Torrance, CA 90501
310-328-0043
-1235-
Solid Waste Association of North America, California Chapters

c/o Gerber and
Associates, 1414 K
Street, Ste. 320
Sacramento, CA 95814
916-446-4656
-1236-
Southeast Asia Business
Council
1946 Embarcadero, Ste.
200
Oakland, CA 94606
510-536-1967
-1237-
Southern California
Association for
Philanthropy
315 West 9th Street,
Ste. 1000
Los Angeles, CA 90015
213-489-7307
-1238-
Southern California
Association of
Nonprofit Housing
3345 Wilshire Blvd.,
Ste. 1000
Los Angeles, CA 90010
213-480-1249
-1239-
Southern California
Auctioneers Association
2702 Ramada Drive
Paso Robles, CA 93446
800-552-0220
-1240-
Southern California
Beverage Network
P.O. Box 17793
Encino, CA 91416
-1241-
Southern California
Broadcasters
Association
5670 Wilshire Blvd.,
Ste. 910
Los Angeles, CA 90036
323-938-3100
-1242-
Southern California
Builders Association
4552 Lincoln Avenue,
Ste. 207
Cypress, CA 90630
714-995-5841
-1243-
Southern California
Contractors'
Association
6055 East Washington
Blvd., Ste. 200
Los Angeles, CA 90040
323-726-3511
-1244-
Southern California
Defense Counsel
888 South Figueroa
Street, 16th Floor
Los Angeles, CA 90017
213-683-3050

-1245-
Southern California
Flower Growers
755 Wall Street
Los Angeles, CA 90014
213-627-2482
-1246-
Southern California
Gardeners Federation
333 South San Pedro
Street
Los Angeles, CA 90013
213-628-1595
-1247-
Southern California
Glass Management
Association
1850 E. 17th Street,
Ste. 103
Santa Ana, CA 92705
714-835-0765
-1248-
Southern California
Golf Association
3740 Cahuenga Blvd.
North Hollywood, CA
91604
818-980-3630
-1249-
Southern California
Marine Association
1006 East Chapman
Avenue
Orange, CA 92866
714-633-7581
-1250-
Southern California
Mechanical Contractors
Association
401 Shatto Place, Ste.
103
Los Angeles, CA 90020
213-738-7950
-1251-
Southern California
Paint and Coating
Association
4885 East 52nd Place
Los Angeles, CA 90040
323-771-3330
-1252-
Southern California
Ready Mixed Concrete
Association
1811 Fair Oaks Avenue
South Pasadena, CA
91030
626-441-3107
-1253-
Southern California
Regional Purchasing
Council
3325 Wilshire Blvd.,
Ste. 604
Los Angeles, CA 90010
213-380-7114
-1254-
Southern California
Restaurant Association

3435 Wilshire Blvd.,
Ste. 2230
Los Angeles, CA 90010
213-384-1200
-1255-
Southern California
Rock Products
Association
P.O. Box 40
South Pasadena, CA
91031
626-441-3107
-1256-
Southern California
School Band and
Orchestra Association
11770 Warner Avenue
Fountain Valley, CA
92708
714-979-2263
-1257-
Southern California
Society of Association
Executives
33 South Catalina
Avenue, Ste. 202
Pasadena, CA 91106
626-449-4270
-1258-
Southern California
Society of Oral and
Maxillofacial Surgeons
2555 Huntington Drive,
Ste. F
San Marino, CA 91108
626-449-6229
-1259-
Southland Farmers'
Market Association
1308 Factory Place,
Ste. 68
Los Angeles , CA 90013
213-244-9190
-1260-
Southland Racing
Association
1826 West St. Andrews
Place
Santa Ana, CA 92704
714-957-2985
-1261-
Specialty Vehicle
Institute of America
2 Jenner Street, Ste.
150
Irvine, CA 92718
949-727-3727
-1262-
Squab Producers of
California
409 Primo Way
Modesto, CA 95358
209-537-4744
-1263-
State Association of
County Auditors
935 14th Street
Marysville, CA 95901
530-741-6412

-1264-
State Association of
County Retirement
Systems
1029 J Street, Ste. 340
Sacramento, CA 95814
916-441-1850
-1265-
State Bar of California
(lawyers)
555 Franklin Street
San Francisco, CA 94102
415-561-8200
-1266-
State Coalition of
Probation Organizations
1211 H Street, Ste. F
Sacramento, CA 95814
916-441-3058
-1267-
State of California
Auto Dismantlers
Association
1900 Point West Way,
Ste. 122
Sacramento, CA 95815
916-924-5232
-1268-
State Restaurant
Association of
California
888-994-2257
-1269-
State Water Contractors
455 Capitol Mall, Ste.
220
Sacramento, CA 95814
916-447-7357
-1270-
Statewide Grocers
Safety Association
1716 X Street
Sacramento, CA 95818
916-444-9807
-1271-
Stockton District
Kidney Bean Growers
P.O. Box 654
Linden, CA 95236
209-887-3420
-1272-
Structural Engineers
Association of Northern
California
74 New Montgomery
Street, Ste. 230
San Francisco, CA 94105
415-974-5147
-1273-
Stucco Manufacturers
Association
2402 Vista Nobleza
Newport Beach, CA 92660
949-640-9902
-1274-
Stuntmen Association of
Motion Pictures
4810 Whitsett Avenue

North Hollywood, CA
91607
818-766-4334
-1275-
Stuntwomen's
Association of Motion
Pictures
P.O. Box 1922
Burbank, CA 91507
818-762-0907
-1276-
Substance Abuse
Librarians and
Information Specialists
P.O. Box 9513
Berkeley, CA 94709
510-642-5208
-1277-
Sufi Psychology
Association
9965 Horn Rood
Sacramento, CA 95827
916-368-6912
-1278-
Sun-Diamond Growers of
California (dried
fruits)
5568 Gibraltar Drive
Pleasanton, CA 94588
925-463-8200
-1279-
Sun-Maid Growers of
California (dried
fruits)
13525 South Bethel
Avenue
Kingsburg, CA 93631
559-896-8000
-1280-
Sunkist Growers (citrus
fruits)
14130 Riverside Drive
Sherman Oaks, CA 91423
818-986-4800
-1281-
Sunsweet Growers
(prunes)
901 North Walton
Yuba City, CA 95993
530-674-5010
-1282-
Surface Technology
Association
P.O. Box 190850
San Francisco, CA 94119
415-399-9702
-1283-
Surplus Line
Association of
California
388 Market Street
San Francisco, CA 94111
415-434-4900
-1284-
Swedish American
Chamber of Commerce of
the Western United
States

564 Market Street, Ste.
305
San Francisco, CA 94104
415-781-4188
-1285-
Sweet Potato Council of
California
P.O. Box 1232
Merced, CA 95340
209-723-3001
-1286-
Swiss American Chamber
of Commerce
P.O. Box 26007
San Francisco, CA 94126
415-433-6679
-1287-
Swiss American Chamber
of Commerce
633 West 5th Street,
64th Floor
Los Angeles, CA 90071
626-974-5429
-1288-
Tavern Guild of San
Francisco
623 Valencia Street
San Francisco, CA 94110
415-861-4910
-1289-
Taxicab Paratransit
Association of
California
1730 I Street, Ste. 240
Sacramento, CA 95814
916-443-5283
-1290-
Technical Securities
Analysts Association
5 Third Street
San Francisco, CA 94103
415-957-1202
-1291-
Telecommunications
Association
74 New Montgomery
Street
San Francisco, CA 94105
415-777-4647
-1292-
Textile Association of
Los Angeles
110 East 9th Street,
Ste. C765
Los Angeles, CA 90079
213-627-6173
-1293-
Thoroughbred Owners of
California
P.O. Box 2608
Del Mar, CA 92014
619-794-1018
-1294-
Tire Retread
Information Bureau
900 Welden Grove
Pacific Grove, CA 93950
408-372-1917
-1295-

Traffic School
Association of
California
1502 West Covina
Parkway, Ste. 112
West Covin, CA 91790
626-962-9466
-1296-

Transaction Processing
Council
c/o Shanley Public
Relations, 777 North
First Street, Ste. 600
San Jose, CA 95112
408-295-8894
-1297-

Transportation
Management Association
9800 S.Sepulveda Blvd.
Los Angeles, CA 90045
310-410-2999
-1298-

Transportation
Management Association
of San Francisco
235 Montgomery Street,
Ste. 1025
San Francisco, CA 94104
415-392-0210
-1299-

U.S. Arab Chamber of
Commerce - Pacific
P.O. Box 422218
San Francisco, CA 94142
415-398-9200
-1300-

U.S. Bangladesh Chamber
of Commerce
3580 Wilshire Blvd.,
17th Floor
Los Angeles, CA 90010
213-383-4722
-1301-

U.S. Council for
International Business
425 California Street,
Ste. 700
San Francisco, CA 94104
415-956-3356
-1302-

U.S. Lifesaving
Association
P.O. Box 366
Huntington Beach, CA
92648
714-968-9360
-1303-

Union of American
Physicians and Dentists
1330 Broadway, Ste. 730
Oakland, CA 94612
510-839-0193
-1304-

United Agribusiness
League
54 Corporate Park
Irvine, CA 92606
949-975-1424
-1305-

United Association of
Equipment Leasing
520 Third Street, Ste.
201
Oakland, CA 94607
510-444-9235
-1306-

United General
Contractors
520 South Virgil Avenue
Los Angeles, CA 90020
213-381-2412
-1307-

United Highway Carriers
Association
1817 South Fresno
Avenue
Stockton, CA 95206
800-483-8343
-1308-

United Hospital
Association
2029 Century Park East,
Ste. 3500
Los Angeles, CA 90069
310-277-7123
-1309-

United Nurses
Association of
California
300 South Park Avenue,
Ste. 840
Pomona, CA 91766
909-620-7749
-1310-

United Nurses of
California
10405 San Diego Mission
Drive, Ste. 106
San Diego, CA 92108
619-280-5401
-1311-

United Ostomy
Association
19772 MacArthur Blvd.,
Ste. 200
Irvine, CA 92612
949-660-8624
-1312-

United States Mexico
Chamber of Commerce
444 South Flower
Street, 9th Floor
Los Angeles, CA 90071
213-623-7725
-1313-

United States Racquet
Stringers Association
P.O. Box 40
Del Mar, CA 92014
619-481-3545
-1314-

United Minority
Business Entrepreneurs
413 Josefa Street
San Jose, CA 95126
408-995-0500
-1315-

University Film and
Video Association
c/o School of Film and
TV
Chapman University
333 N. Glassell Street
Orange, CA 92866
714-997-6765
-1316-

Valley International
Trade Association
P.O. Box 591
Woodland Hills, CA
91365
818-346-5620
-1317-

Vegetable Bargaining
Association of
California
P.O. Box 519
Greenfield, CA 93927
831-674-5547
-1318-

Video Electronics
Standards Association
2150 North First
Street, Ste. 440
San Jose, CA 95131
408-435-0333
-1319-

Video Software Dealers
Association
16530 Ventura Blvd.
Ste. 400
Encino, CA 91436
818-385-1500
-1320-

Voluntary Plan
Administrators
23622 Calabasa Road,
Ste. 250
Calabasas, CA 91372
818-591-9444
-1321-

Walnut Bargaining
Association
1225 H Street
Sacramento, CA 95814
916-645-8835
-1322-

Walnut Marketing Board
1540 River Park Drive,
Ste. 203
Sacramento, CA 95815
916-922-5888
-1323-

WateReuse Association
915 L Street, Ste. 1000
Sacramento, CA 95814
916-442-2746
-1324-

Wedding and Portrait
Photographers
International
P.O. Box 2003
Santa Monica, CA 90406
310-451-0090
-1325-

West Coast Book People
Association
27 McNear Drive
San Rafael, CA 94901
415-459-1227
-1326-

Western Agricultural
Chemicals Association
3835 North Freeway
Blvd., Ste. 140
Sacramento, CA 95834
916-568-3660
-1327-

Western Apicultural
Society of North
America (bees and
honey)
2110 X Street
Sacramento, CA 95818
916-451-2337
-1328-

Western Arts Alliance
(performing arts)
44 Page Street, Ste.
604B
San Francisco, CA 94102
415-621-4400
-1329-

Western Association of
Chamber of Commerce
Executives
P.O. Box 1736
Sacramento, CA 95812
916-442-2223
-1330-

Western Association of
Convention and Visitors
Bureaus
1730 I Street, Ste. 240
Sacramento, CA 95814
916-443-9012
-1331-

Western Association of
Equipment Lessors
520 3rd Street, Ste.
201
Oakland, CA 94607
510-444-9235
-1332-

Western Association of
Schools and Colleges
P.O. Box 9990, Mills
College
Oakland, CA 94613
510-632-5000
-1333-

Western Association of
Venture Capitalists
3000 Sand Hill Road,
Building 1, Ste. 190
Menlo Park, CA 94025
650-854-1322
-1334-

Western Brahman
Breeders Association
P.O. Box 1012
Oakdale, CA 95361
209-376-2304
-1335-

Western Crop Protection
Association
3835 N. Freeway Blvd.
Sacramento, CA 95834
916-568-3660
-1336-

Western Economic
Association
International
7400 Center Avenue,
Ste. 109
Huntington Beach, CA
92647
714-898-3222
-1337-

Western Electrical
Contractors Association
7500 14th Avenue, Ste.
25
Sacramento, CA 95820
916-453-0112
-1338-

Western Fairs
Association
1776 Tribute Road, Ste.
210
Sacramento, CA 95815
916-927-3100
-1339-

Western Growers
Association
1005 12th Street, Ste.
A
Sacramento, CA 95814
916-446-1435
-1340-

Western Growers
Association
4991 E. McKinley Avenue
Fresno, CA 93727
559-454-0507
-1341-

Western League of
Savings Institutions
925 L Street, Ste. 300
Sacramento, CA 95814
916-443-5955
-1342-

Western League of
Savings Institutions
9841 Airport Blvd.,
Ste. 418
Los Angeles, CA 90045
310-348-7700
-1343-

Western Maquiladora
Trade Association
(manufacturing plants
along the Mexican
border)
San Diego
619-234-9682
-1344-

Western Marine
Association
P.O. Box 1847
Stockton, CA 95201
209-466-1414
-1345-

Western Marine Safety
Service Association
P.O. Box 1847
Stockton, CA 95201
209-466-1414
-1346-

Western Mobilehome
Parkowners Association
455 Capitol Mall, Ste.
800
Sacramento, CA 95814
916-448-7002
-1347-

Western Mobilehome
Parkowners Association
3530 Camino Del Rio
North, Ste. 203
San Diego, CA 92108
619-285-1401
-1348-

Western Motor Carriers
8 Crow Canyon Court,
Ste. 210
San Ramon, CA 94507
925-838-5850
-1349-

Western Occupational
and Environmental
Medical Association
74 New Montgomery
Street, Ste. 230
San Francisco, CA 94105
415-764-4803
-1350-

Western Packaging
Association
878 Hillcrest Drive
Redwood City, CA 94062
650-599-9959
-1351-

Western Payments
Alliance
1111 Bayhill Drive,
Ste. 150
San Bruno, CA 94066
650-871-8762
-1352-

Western Pension and
Benefits Conference,
Los Angeles Chapter
1804 West Burbank Blvd.
Burbank, CA 91506
818-846-1129
-1353-

Western Propane Gas
Association
2131 Capitol Avenue
Sacramento, CA 95816
916-447-9742
-1354-

Western Range
Association (wool
growers)
6060 Sunrise Vista
Drive, Ste. 2400
Citrus Heights, CA
95610
916-962-1500
-1355-

Western Service Workers
Association
1666 7th Street
Oakland, CA 94607
510-832-2111
-1356-
Western Society of Weed
Science
P.O. Box 963
Newark, CA 94560
510-790-1252
-1357-
Western States
Advertising Agents
Association
6404 Wilshire Blvd.,
Ste. 1111
Los Angeles, CA 90048
323-655-1951
-1358-
Western States
Petroleum Association
505 North Brand Blvd.,
Ste. 1400
Glendale, CA 91203
818-545-4105
-1359-
Western Suppliers
Association
1777 Borel Place, Ste.
204
San Mateo, CA 94402
650-341-7222
-1360-
Western United Dairymen
1315 K Street
Modesto, CA 95354
209-527-6453
-1361-
Western Wall and
Ceiling Contractors
Association
2286 N. State College
Blvd.
Fullerton, CA 92831
714-256-1244
-1362-
Western Wood Products
Association
522 SW 5th Ave., Ste.
500
Portland, OR 97204
503-224-3930
-1363-
Wine and Spirits
Wholesalers of
California
4549 Jubilio Drive
Tarzana, CA 91356
818-774-0996
-1364-
Wine Institute
425 Market Street, Ste.
1000
San Francisco, CA 94105
415-512-0151
-1365-
Women in Architecture
P.O. Box 84924

San Diego, CA 92138
619-338-4199
-1366-
Women in Business
610 W. Ash Street
San Diego, CA 92101
619-525-2637
-1367-
Women in Film
6464 Sunset Blvd., Ste.
1080
Hollywood, CA 90028
323-463-6040
-1368-
Woodwork Institute of
California
3164 Industrial Blvd.
West Sacramento, CA
95691
916-372-9943
-1369-
World Floor Covering
Association
2211 East Howell Avenue
Anaheim, CA 92806
714-978-6440
-1370-
World International
Nail and Beauty
Association
1221 North Lake View
Anaheim, CA 92807
714-779-9883
-1371-
World Trade Club
Ferry Building, Rm. 300
San Francisco, CA 94111
415-981-1237
-1372-
World Wide Pet Supply
Association
406 South First Avenue
Arcadia, CA 91006
626-447-2222
-1373-
Writers Guild of
America West (film,
television, and radio
writers)
7000 W. Third Street
Los Angeles, CA 90048
323-951-4000
-1374-
Young Executives of
America
180 Newport Center
Drive
Newport Beach, CA 92660
949-759-5456
-1375-
Young Musicians
Foundation
195 S. Beverly Blvd.,
Ste. 414
Beverly Hills, CA 90212
310-859-7668

Notes

Notes

Index

This is an index of key words and subjects. References are to *entry numbers*, not pages.

-A-

Accordion players, 6
Accountants, 1221
- black, 1017
- certified public, 692, 693
- chartered certified, 187
- independent, 336
- management, 919
- women, 121

Acting coaches and teachers, 1102
Actors, 7
- screen, 1201

Acupuncture, 26, 161, 205, 273, 816
Administrators, 930
- adult education, 275
- college, 171
- legal, 206
- public, 374, 710
- state and federal education programs, 303
- vocational, 399

Adoption lawyers, 2
Adult business, 8, 274
Advertisers and advertising, 9-12, 31, 42, 237, 1185, 1357
- outdoor, 724

Advocates, governmental, 917
Aerobics, 13
Aeronautics, 80
African American. See Black
Agents
- enrolled, 694
- free, 1022
- general, 32, 978
- manufacturers,
- talent, 219

Aging, 122, 307
- homes for the, 334

Agriculture and agricultural, 14, 514, 929, 1304, 1339, 1340
- aircraft, 276
- chemicals, 1326

- commissioners, 277
- energy, 15
- marketing, 1015
- production consultants, 278
- teachers, 279
- women, 761

Air conditioning, 16, 918, 1206, 1207
Air pollution, 280
Alarm, 281, 409
Alcohol and alcoholism
- counselors, 306
- drinking driver treatment, 324
- and drug programs, 304, 819
- recovery homes, 305
- substance abuse librarians, 572

Alfalfa seed, 775
Almond, 23, 247
Ambulance, 33, 282
Analysts
- financial, 981
- institutional, 923
- Jungian, 956
- security, 1202, 1290

Anaplastology, 34
Andrology, 104
Anesthesiologists, 690
Antique appraisal, 129
Apartment, 130-135, 284, 1173, 1186
- owners

Apiculture, 1327
Apple, 286
Appraisers, 105
- antique, 129
- biological collections, 169
- fee, 1024
- real estate, 1071
- rural, 112

Apricot, 137
Aquaculture, 288, 289
Aquariums, 403
Arab, 1299
Archaeology, 1213
Architectural manufacturers, 35

Architects, 81-83, 111
- Landscape, 114
- women, 1365

Archivists, 208
Armenian, 138
Arson investigators, 464
Artichoke, 139, 291, 292
Artificial intelligence, 36
Art and artists 463
- digital, 932
- graphic, 84, 886
- performing, 1328

Asia, Southeast, 703, 1236
Asian and Pacific, higher education, 143
Asian-American, 703. See also specific groups
- architects and engineers, 140
- business, 144
- educators, 143
- journalists, 141
- manufacturers, 142

Asparagus, 293
Asphalt, 145, 1079
Assisted living, 294
Association executives, 106, 691, 1090, 1257, 1329
Associations
- community, 794
- industrial, 241

Astronautics, 80
Astronomical, 225
Athletic trainers, 404
Attorneys. See Lawyers
Auction, auto, 407
Auctioneers, 711, 1239
Audio publishers, 226
Auditors, county, 1263
Australia, 227
Authors. See Writers
Automatic merchandising, 410, 1043
Automobile and automotive, 229, 234
- autobody, 408

- collision repair, 1223
- dealers, 308, 596, 903, 1076
- dismantlers, 1267
- racing writers-broadcasters, 46
- renting and leasing, 771
- repair, 230
- service, 231, 232
- teachers, 1078
- wholesalers, 411

Aviation
- agricultural, 276
- business, 412
- naval, 209

Avocado, 413

-B-

Bail agents, 414
Bail insurance, 415
Bangladesh, 1300
Banks and bankers
- clearinghouse, 417
- community, 795
- independent community, 905
- industrial, 339

Bar associations. See Lawyers
Bean,
- dry, 503, 842
- kidney, 1271
- growers, 419
- shippers, 420

Beauty, 421, 1370
Beef, 422
Beekeepers, 712, 1327
Beer wholesalers, 423
Beets, sugar, 424
Behavior analysis, 309
Benefit plans, 1352
Beverage, 423, 573, 873, 1240
- merchants, 425
- soft drink

Bicycle dealers, 1044
Bioanalysts, 310
Biomedical, 426, 427
- engineering, 244
- industry, 243

Black
- accountants, 1017
- Chamber of Commerce, 887
- data processing, 246
- engineers, 1080
- entertainment, 19
- lawyers, 245
- nurses, 1170

- police, 1171
- public relations, 1045
- social workers, 311

Book. See also Writers
- reviewers, 238
- publicists, 248
- publishers, 1325
- production, 249

Botanical, 428
Brahman breeders, 1334
Brewers, 685
British, 250
Broadcasters, 1116, 1241
- auto racing, 46

Buckskin, 49
Builders, 146-148, 251, 252, 1107, 1242
Building, 253, 430, 431
- credit, 254, 255
- officials, 432, 938
- owners and managers, 256-260

Bulgarian, 261
Bus, 433
- school, 669

Business, 263, 434, 435, 973, 999
- brokers, 312
- independent, 337
- marketing, 264
- properties, 436
- publications, 168
- services, 50
- small, 684, 686, 1211
- for social responsibility, 262
- women, 51

-C-

Canadian, 769
Cantaloupe, 439, 770
Car. See Automobile
Cardiology, 56
Career
- education, 37
- and planning,
Carrot, 530
Cartridge remanufacturers, 170
Casino executives, 1047
Cattle, 441, 601, 767, 1334
CD-ROM producers, 314
Ceiling contractors, 754
Cement, 442, 443

Cemeteries, 928
Chambers of commerce. See note at 445. Use key word.
- Executives, 1329

Check cashers, 447
Cheese, 448
Chefs, 777
Chemical, 52, 778
- agricultural, 1326

Cherry, 449
Child victim treatment centers, 188
Children's
- homes, 315
- hospitals, 450
- services, 389

Chinese, 780, 782, 783
Chiropractic, 451, 937
- orthopedists, 57

Chlorinators, gas, 1023
Christian
- educators, 784
- schools, 189

Christmas tree growers, 452
Chrysanthemum growers, 453
Churches, 478
Cigar, 454
Cinematographers, 107
Citrus fruit, 290
Classrooms, relocatable, 302
Cleaners, 455-512
Cleaning employees, 191
Clerks
- city, 786
- municipal, 942

Club, 713
Coffee, 1108
Coin machine. See automated merchandising
Collectors, 316
College
- accreditation, 1332
- art and design, 203
- community, 797
- community, administrators, 171
- community, faculty, 861
- community, journalism, 796
- independent, 202, 904

Collision repair, 1223
Communications
- audiovisual, 933

- business, 934
Community action, 265
Composers, 116, 1019
Computer, 1172
- Consultant, 1020
- Internet, 204
- operations, 162
- middleware, 944
- simulation, 1214
- training, 193
- software, 1234
Concrete, 1252
- contractors, 462
- masonry, 801
- precast, 636
Conservation corps, 349
Conservators, public, 710
Construction, 466
- crime prevention, 803
- legislative council, 804
- materials, 806
- managers, 172
- research, 805
- specifications, 807
- women in, 1041
Consultants, 1046, 1136
Consumer products, 812
Contractors, 146-148, 813, 814, 1243; see also Construction
- building service, 1106
- concrete, 462
- electrical, 845-847, 1051-1054, 1337
- engineering, 853-855
- general, 151-154, 1306
- insulation, 924
- mechanical, 1250
- roofing, 157, 158
- tile, 160
- wall and ceiling, 1361
- water, 1269
Convention bureaus, 1330
Coroners, 714
Corporate growth, 163
Correctional officers, 639
Corrections, 470
- mental health, 45
- research and information, 164
Cosmetologists, 471
Cotton, 815

- ginners, 472
- growers, 473
Councils of governments, 318
Counseling and development, 296
County. See key word
Court
- clerks, 480
- reporters, 481
Crab boat owners, 823
Crane, 824
Creamery operators, 482
Credit, 73, 1158
- bureaus, 150
Credit union, 483, 1021
- information technologies, 913
- marketing, 825
- postal, 1049
Crime prevention, 1042
Criminal justice, 55
Crop improvement, 484
Crop protection, 1335
Crystals, 38
Customs brokers. 827, 828

-D-

Dairy, 155, 829, 830, 1360; see also Milk
- herd improvement, 486
- research, 487
Dance, 298
Data processing
- blacks, 246
- management, 831
Dates, 488, 489
Dental and dentists, 492, 1188, 1303
- assistants, 491
- hygienists, 493
- laboratory, 494, 832
- managed care, 321
- plans, 322
- Seventh Day Adventist, 1032
Dermatology, 497
Desalting, 67
Design, 211
Dichondra, 835
Dietetic, 499
Direct marketing, 1177, 836, 837
Directors, 838
Distributors, 500
District attorneys, 501
Diving equipment, 839
Down, 68
Drama, 24

Drinking driver treatment, 324
Drug abuse
- counselors, 306
- librarians, 572
- programs. 819
Drum reconditioners, 502
Drywall, 1161

-E-

Economic, 239, 1114, 1336
Education, 1050, 1178
- administrators, state and federal programs, 303
- adult, 474
- adult, administrators, 275
- bilingual, 295
- childhood, 1137
- continuation, 467
- Evangelical Lutheran, 859
- higher, 269
- higher, physical education, 1016
- history, 1215
- private, specialized, 368
Educators, 1139; see also Teachers
- jail, 341
- marine, 1064
- work experience, 402
Egg, 505, 1114a
Elected officials, women, 506
Electrical
- contractors, 845-7, 1051-54, 1189, 1337
- and gas industries, 843
- training, 848
Electronic, 69-72
- design automation, 851
- document systems, 849
- representatives, 850
Emissions testing, 508
Employees. See also type
- benefit planning, 852
- state, 715, 716
Employers, 325, 326

• organizations, 369
Employment lawyers, 1055
Energy
  • agricultural, 15
  • geothermal, 881
  • managers, 212
  • pool and spa, 704
  • officials, 173
  • producers, independent, 906
  • solar, 702, 1092
Engineering and engineers, 571, 701, 857
  • and architects, 856
  • black, 1080
  • in California government, 1140
  • civil, 108, 109,
  • consulting, 808
  • electronic and electrical, 914
  • Latino, 1228
  • material and process, 1220
  • mechanical, 115
  • plumbing, 119
  • structural, 1272
Enology, 101
Enrolled agents, 694
Entertainment technicians, 19
Entrepreneurs, 240; see also Business
Environmental
  • health, 327
  • professionals, 201
Equipment leasing, 1305, 1331
Escrow, 511, 858
Examiners, document, 1012
Exchange
  • accommodators, 864
  • carriers, 1056
Executive, 860; see also type
  • women, 865
  • young, 1374
Exercise, 13, 65, 900

-F-

Fabricare, 512
Faculty
  • California State University, 513
  • community college, 861
  • University of California, 818

Fairs, racing, 406
Farm. See also Agriculture
  • advisors, 328
  • managers, 112
Farmers, 720, 1057
  • market, 1259
  • Nisei, 1077
  • organic, 444
Fashion, 515, 862, 1190
Feathers, 68
Fence, 517
Fiduciary, 1141
Fertilizer, 518
Fig, 519, 520
Film. See also Motion picture
Film extruders and converters, 521
Film and tape, 75, 1315
Finance and financial
  • community, service, 798
  • commercial, 793
  • executives, 866
  • institutions, 867
  • planners, 931
  • premium, 637
  • services, 522, 523, 1226
  • women, 869
Fire and firefighters
  • chiefs, 524
  • Dept. of Forestry employees, 495
  • districts, 870
  • firefighters, 717
  • rescue, 871
  • retired, 980
Fish and fishers, 676
  • fisheries, 525
  • fishermen, 1109
  • tuna, 126
  • salmon, 667
Fisheries, 525
Fitness. See Exercise
Flash, compact, 800
Floor covering, 872, 1369
Floral, 526, 718
Flowers
  • cut, 485
  • growers, 1245
Flute, 1060
Food, 873, 1195
  • frozen, 74
  • nutritional, 1066
  • processors, 566
  • service, women, 1165
  • technologists, 915, 916
  • and wine, 85

Football coaches, community college, 460
Forests and forestry, 528
  • employees, 495
  • foresters, 574
  • landowners, 875
  • products, 527
  • women, 762
Foster parents, 719
French, 877, 878
Frozen food, 74
Fruit
  • citrus, 1280
  • dried, 840, 1278, 1279
  • rare, 650
  • stone, 727
  • tree, 536
Fund raising executives, 1070
Funeral
  • directors, 531, 532
  • motorcycle escort, 1006
Furnishings, home, 896
Fuyu growers, 533

-G-

Garden equipment, 968
Gardeners, 1246
Garment contractors, 880
Gas, 802, 1110
  • chlorinators, 1023
  • industry, 843
  • propane, 1353
Gay, business people, 883
Geologists, engineering, 198-200
Geothermal energy, 881
German, 882
Glass, 1247
Golf and golfers, 1082, 1248
  • course superintendents, 534
  • golfers, 1088, 1142
  • indoor, 912
  • public links, 1149
Grain and feed, 535
Grape
  • desert, 498
  • growers, 536
  • winegrape growers, 401, 1011
Graphics and graphic artists, 84

Grocery and grocers, 537, 1084
- Latino, 1000
- manufacturers, 889
- safety, 1270

Groundwater, 1339, 1340
Guardians, public, 374
Guard, National, 1061
Guard, security, 345, 468
Gynecology and gynecologists, 59
- laparoscopists, 44

Gynecology, 59

-H-

Handwriting analysis, 76
Harbor masters, 329
Harbors, 584
Harp, 77
Hay growers, 1198
Hazardous waste, 541
Health, 298, 891; see also Medicine, Mental health
- care quality, 297
- care districts, 174
- environmental, 327
- executives, county, 820
- information, 543
- facilities, 330
- plans, 331, 390
- officers, 890
- orthomolecular, 1219
- services at home, 299
- underwirters, 332

Hearing reporters, 391
Heating, 569, 918; see also Air conditioning
Hereford, 601, 767
Highway
- carriers, 1307
- patrolmen, 333

Hispanic. See Latino
Home furnishings, 896
Home warranty, 897
Horse
- buckskin, 49
- harness, 540,
- quarter, 1111
- thoroughbred, 739, 1293

Horsemen, 721
Hospice, 722
Hospital, 542, 1308
- Catholic, 313
- public, 375

Hospitality industry, 898
Hotel, 545, 899, 1192
Housing, 547
- authorities, 546
- finance agencies, 350
- manufactured, 580
- nonprofit, 1238

Human resources, 1085, 1145, 1216
Hypnosis, 78
Hypnotists, examiners, 64

-I-

Ice cream vendors, 335
Image industry, 902
Incontinent product suppliers, 548
Industrial
- associations, 241
- office parks, 1026
- real estate, 79

Information
- consultants, 1059
- display, 1217

Insect ecologists, 167
Insurance, 18, 86, 555
- adjustors, 338
- agents, 925-927, 1143
- agents and brokers, 907
- companies, 175
- health, 176, 332
- independent, 1025
- liability, 370
- life, 176, 346, 1168
- personal, 1123
- self, 678
- wholesalers, 556

Interior design, 475, 570
Interlock service, 340
Interment, 928
International business, 1301. See also Trade, international
Internet, 204, 557
Investigators, 553
- arson, 464
- credit card, 935
- licensed, 343
- state, 392

Investment, realty, 1156
Iranian, 1229
Irrigation consultants, 113

-J-

Japan
- business, 953
- Chamber of Commerce, 954, 955

Japanese-American farmers, 1077
Jewelers, 969
Joint powers authorities, 342
Journalism. See Press, Broadcasting, Radio, Television
Judges, 559
- administrative law, 181

Jungian analysts, 956

-K-

Kiwifruit, 560, 957, 958
Korean
- businessmen, 961
- Chamber of Commerce, 963
- dry cleaners, 964
- grocers, 959
- investors and traders, 965
- medicine and acupuncture, 205
- women artists and writers, 960

-L-

Laboratory
- clinical, 457
- medical, 300
- public health, 1148

Land surveyors, 561
Land title, 562
Landscape
- architects, 114
- contractors, 563

Language, general semantics, 948
Laporoscopists, gynecological, 44
Lath and plaster, 941
Latino
- business. 892, 967
- chambers of commerce, 544, 893, 1191
- dental, 966
- engineers, 1228
- grocers, 1000
- philanthropy, 894

Lawyers, 235, 236, 975, 1062, 1174, 1265
- adoption, 2
- applicants', 287
- appellate, defense, 285
- for the arts, 565
- black, 245
- comprehensive defense, 461
- concerned, 788, 789
- consumer, 809-811
- criminal, 47
- for criminal justice, 405
- defense, 194, 195, 218, 490, 1244
- employment, 1055
- railroad, 1030
- state, 181
- trial, 62, 1197
- trust and estate, 63
- women, 763

Legal
- administrators, 206
- assistants, 1187
- secretaries, 1179

Lesbian businesswomen, 883
Lettuce, 901
Libraries and librarians, 572
- law, 817
- school, 673
- substance abuse, 1276

Life underwriters, 970, 972
Lifesaving, 1302
Limes, 347
Limousine, 576
Livestock, 1135
Llama, 943
Loan dealers, collateral, 792
Lobbyists, 917
Local agency formation commissions, 348
Locksmiths, 577
Lodging industry, 578
Loggers, 149
Luggage, 87
Lumber, 984, 1180

-M-

Macadamia, 579
Magazines, 785, 985
Magnetic resonance, 1230

Maintenance, 908
Management, 723, 1063
Managers, 317, 351, 978
Manufacturers, 581, 999, 1027, 1209
- agents, 986

Maquiladora, 1343
Marina, 988
Marine, 583, 1086, 1249, 1344
- educators, 1064
- parks, 584
- safety, 1345

Marine corps
- aviation, 989
- drill instructors, 990

Marketing, 88, 264, 983, 991, 1166, 1177
- agricultural, 1081
- direct, 1081
- executives, 1167
- multi-level, 1009
- professional services, 1218
- promotional, 1146
- publishers, 1150
- telemarketing, 125

Markets, farmers, 1259
Marshals, 992
Masonry, 993, 801, 993, 994
Massage, sports, 949
Meat , 1065
Media, 995
Medicine and medical, 55, 971; see also specialties
- concerned, 790
- critical care, 1224
- directors, 353
- environmental, 1349
- equine sports, 165
- group, 89
- industrial, 696
- Korean, 205
- oriental, 688, 698, 816
- internal, 697
- marketing, 996
- occupational, 1349
- product suppliers, 354
- sports, 123
- supplies, disposable, 987
- transcription, 39
- transportation, 588

- veterinary. See Veterinary medicine

Meeting planners, 997, 998
Mental health, 552
- agencies, 192, 479
- corrections, 45
- directors, 589

Metal, cast, 440
Mexican, 1312. See also Latino
Microenterprise, 301
Middleware, 944
Milk; see also Dairy
- manufactured, 582
- product, 776
- producers, 21, 1001

Mining, 590
Minority business entrepreneurs, 1314
Mobilehome parkowners, 591, 1346, 1347
Mortgage, 592
- bankers, 593
- brokers, 355

Mortuary, 594
Mosquito control, 595, 1002
Motel, 130, 545
Motion picture, 945, 1004, 1315
- archivists, 208
- art directors, 1231
- arts and sciences, 4
- cinematographers, 107
- credit, 1003
- documentary, 940
- editors, 54
- export, 1005
- laboratories, 190
- marketing, 75
- producers, 20
- stuntmen, 1274
- stuntwomen, 1275
- writers, 1373

Motorcycle, 1007
- funeral escort, 1006
- safety, 1008

Moving and storage, 597
Mules, 90
Mushroom, 7010
Music, 979
- arrangers, 116
- composers, 116
- country, 3
- merchants, 1028

- young musicians, 1375

Mustang, 91

-N-

Nail and beauty, 1370
Narcotic officers, 600
National Guard, 1061
Navy, 209
Neurologists, 177
News
- ombudsmen, 1101
- radio and television, 1153

Newspaper publishers, 603
Nonprofits, 358
Numismatics, 1144
Nurserymen, 360
Nurses, 604, 607, 1309, 1310
- anesthetists, 359
- black, 1170
- critical care, 43
- for ethical standards, 608
- occupational health, 709
- ophthalmic registered, 118
- practitioners, 458
- vocational, 575

Nuts, 840

-O-

Obstetricians, 59
Obstetricians and gynecologists (ob-gyn), 59, 361, 1087, 1096
Occupational
- centers, 380
- health nurses, 709
- therapy, 1097

Ocularists, 117
Oil, 551, 802, 1358
- independent producers, 909
- independent refiners, 787
- independent marketers, 550

Olive, 609, 610, 1099
Ophthalmic
- outpatient surgery, 1104
- photographers, 1100
- registered nurses, 118

Ophthalmology, 27, 220, 270, 362
- pediatric, 40
- professors, 223

Optical laboratories, 611
Optometric, 612
Organic food, 444
Organization development, 242
Orthodontics, 726, 1113
Orthopedic medicine, 614
- chiropractic, 57
- podiatric, 48

Osteopathic medicine
- occupational and preventive, 92
- physicians and surgeons, 1103
- state executive directors, 210

Ostomy, 1311
Ostrich, 615
Oxygen, 1105

-P-

Packaging, 1350
Pain management, 28, 558
Paint, 616, 1251
Painting and decorating contractors, 1118, 1119
Pancreatic, 93
Park and recreation, 379, 617, 618
Parking, 1120
- public, 646

Parliamentarians, 364
Parole, 639
Pathologists, 699
- speech, 708

Payments, 1351
Peace officers, 619, 977
- for justice, 1098
- research, 1121

Peach, 620
- canning, 438
- cling, 456
- freestone, 529

Pear, 621, 622
Pecan, 623
Pediatric, 29, 30
- neurosurgery, 102
- ophthalmology, 40

Pension, 1352
Pepper, 624
Persimmons, fuyu, 533
Personal communications, 22

Personnel. See Human resources
- school administrators,

Pest control operators, 1124
Petroleum. See Oil and Gas
Pet supply, 1372
Pharmacists, 625
- employee, 509
- health system, 695

Philanthropy, 1083, 1237
- Latino, 894

Photocopiers, 365
Photographers
- advertising, 12
- ophthamalic, 1100
- wedding and portrait, 1324

Physical education, 298
Physical therapy, 94
Physician assistants, 271
Physicians, 626, 1303
- dispensing, 323
- emergency, 58
- family, 268
- naturopathic, 356

Pilots, 627
- test, 1225

Pistachio, 628
Planning, 96
Plaster, 941, 1125
Plastic surgery, 100
Plum, 629
Plumbing, 119, 569, 1126
- contractors, 630-631
- contractors, heating and cooling, 1127
- mechanical officials, 936

Podiatric, 632
- dermatology, executives, 120
- orthopedics, 48

Police, 613, 1193
- black, 1171
- chiefs, 633
- rescue, 871
- retired, 980

Pool, 704
Ports, 366, 884
- Port captains, 329

Pork, 634
Post-secondary schools, private, 367
Poultry, 635
- squab, 1262

Power sources, 1128
Press, 888, 910, 1129, 1181
Pretrial services, 1029
Primary care, 638
Printing, 1130-1132
Probation, 639, 1266
- officers, 779
- Process servers, 365
Produce, 156, 879, 1194
Producer-handler, 641
Producers, films, 1134
Production and inventory control, 97
Professors. See also Faaculty
- California State University, 182
- ophthalmology, 223
Propane gas, 1353
Prosthodontics, 25
Prune, 642, 1147, 1281
Psychiatry and psychiatrists, 60, 643, 1089
- technicians, 373
- child and adolescent, 266
Psychology and psychologists, 644, 1182
- humanistic, 166
- Jungian, 956
- school, 388
- Sufi, 1277
- Transactional, 952
Psychometrics, school, 388
Public
- administrators, 374
- conservators, 710
- defenders, 645
- guardians, 374
Public health laboratory, 1148
Public relations, 1045
Publications, business, 168
Publishers
- audio, 226
- book, 1325
- desktop, 196
- marketing, 1150
Purchasing, 1253
- management, 1151, 1152

-Q-

Quarter horse, 1111

-R-

Racing, 398, 1260
- fairs, 406
Racquet stringers, 1313
Radio, 895, 1153
Radiological, 649
Railroad
- lawyers, 1030
- short line, 682
Raisin, 1154-1155
Reactors, 1067
Real estate
- appraisers, 1071
- brokers, 377
- industrial, 79
- investment, 1156
- management, 921
- Realtors, 378
Reconditioners, drum, 502
Recording arts and sciences, 1013
Recorder, county, 821
Records, law enforcement, 564
Recreation, 298
- and park, 379
- vehicle, 651
Recycling, scrap, 922
Redevelopment, 652
Redwood, 653
Refiners, 787
Refuse removal, 654
Regional center agencies, 213
Rehabilitation, 382, 383, 655
Remodeling industry, 1037
Renderers, 1112
Rental, 372, 1160
Reporters (legal)
- deposition, 833
- training schools, 214, 215
Repossessors, 344
Residential care homes, 799
Resource conservation districts, 384
Resource recovery, 657
Respiratory care, 689
Restaurant, 435, 658, 659, 885, 1183, 1196, 1254, 1268
Retail, 660, 661, 911
Retired. See type of employee
Retirement systems, 376, 1264
Rice, 663
- growers, 1163

- promotion, 664
Right-of-way, 947
Rock products, 1175, 1255
Roofing, 665
- contractors, 157, 158, 1164, 1184

-S-

Safety
- employees, 751
- grocers, 1270
- traffic, 184
Sales. See Marketing
Salmon, 667
Sanitation agencies, 385
Savings institutions, 1341, 1342
Scaffold, 1199
Scholars, 386
- independent, 1048
School. See also Schools (for types of institutions)
- accreditation, 1332
- administrators, 178-180
- band and orchestra, 1256
- boards, 668, 1069
- bus, 669
- business officials, 387
- districts, small, 1212
- districts, suburban, 393
- districts, urban, 185
- employees, 670
- facility manufacturers, 1200
- food service, 671, 672
- nurses, 674
- psychologists and psychometrists, 388
Schools. See also School
- Augustinian,
- Christian, 189
- driving, 841
- high schools, 567
- low-wealth, 207
- middle schools, 568
- prison-impacted, 791

- private post-secondary, 367
- reporter training, 214, 215
- traffic, 744, 1295

Science and scientists, 41, 371
Scrap, 922
Seafood, 525, 676
Sealers, of weights and measures, 277
Secondhand dealers, 792
Secretaries, legal, 1179
Securities
- dealers, 1031
- public, 647, 648

Security agencies, 345
Security analysts, 1202, 1290
Seed, 677
Seismological, 1203
Self insurers, 678
Semantics, general, 948
Semi-conductor, 1204, 1205
Seminar leaders, 98
Separation science, 679
Service station, 680
Service workers, 1355
Sheep. See Wool
Sheet metal, 681, 1206-1208
Sheriffs, 613, 725
Shipping, 1115
Shopping centers, 939
Sightseeing, 99
Sign, electric, 507
Singapore, 1210
Singers, 1232
Ski industry, 683
Small business, 684, 686, 1211
Social studies, 477
Social work and social workers, 1033, 1034
- black, 311
- clinical, 687

Soft drink, 602, 768
Software, 1234
Solid waste, 1235
Southeast Asian, 703, 1236
Spa, 704
Space, 705
Special district, 706
Speech, 707
- pathologists, 708
- religious, 1159

Sports
- medicine, 123
- medicine, equine sports, 165

Squab, 1262
Statistics, mathematical, 920
Storage, 597
Store fixtures, 1072
Strawberry, 728, 1133
Stress management, 950
Stucco, 1273
Stuntmen, 1274
Stuntwomen, 1275
Subcontractors, 124
Suppliers, 1359
Surety, 183, 729
Surface technology, 1282
Surgery and surgeons, 61
- ambulatory, 283
- cosmetic, 267
- graduate, 1227
- industrial, 696
- neurological, 357
- oral and maxillofacial, 363, 1091, 1258
- pediatic neurosurgery, 102
- plastic, 160, 700

Surplus, 159, 1283
Surrogates, 946
Surveyors, land, 561
Swap meet, 730
Swedish, 1284
Sweet potato, 731, 1285
Swiss, 1286, 1287

-T-

Talent agents, 219
Tavern, 1093, 1288
Tax collectors, county, 319
Taxicab paratransit, 1289
Teachers, 465, 733-735; see also Educators
- automotive, 1078
- of English, 394
- of English to speakers of other languages (TESOL), 395
- retired, 1068
- science, 675

Technology, 136, 705
Teleservices, 125
Telephone, 736
- cellular, carriers, 773

Television, 895
- arts and sciences, 5, 1014
- cable, 437

- news, 1153
- program executives, 1035

Temporary services, 396, 397
Textiles, 1292
Textile dyers, 221
Theatre owners, 1036
Therapy
- educational, 197
- marriage and family, 352
- Thoracic, 737

Thoroughbred owners, 1293
Threat assessment, 222
Tile, 160, 774
Tire
- dealers, 740
- retread, 1294

Tomato, 741, 742
- processing, 640

Tow truck, 743
Trade, international, 476, 874, 951, 1095, 1316, 1343, 1371
Traffic safety educators, 184
Traffic schools, 744, 1295
Training and development, 103
Transaction processing, 1296
Transactional analysis, 952
Transit, 745
Transmission rebuilders, 228
Transportation, 745
- management, 1297, 1298

Travel, 746
- business, 974, 1018
- organizations, 459
- parks, 747

Treasurers, county, 319
Trucks and trucking
- dump truck owners, 504
- renting, 771
- trucking, 748, 1074, 1307, 1348

Trustees, 749
Tunaboat, 126

-U-

Universities, independent, 202
University faculty. See Faculty

Upholsterers, custom,
826
Urological, 752
Utilities, municipal,
598

–V–

Vector control. See
Mosquito
Vegetable, 1317
Vehicle,
 • electric, 844
 • leasing, 1073
 • recreation, 1157
 • specialty, 1261
Vendors, automatic.
 See automatic
 merchandising
Venture capitalists,
1333
Vesselite
 practitioners, 272
Veterans service
 officers, 320
Veterinary medicine,
753, 1176
Video, 1315
 • adult, 8
 • electronic, 1318
 • laboratory, 190
 • software, 1319
Vineyard, 127
Viticulture, 101
Vocational
 administrators, 399
Voluntary plans, 1320

–W–

Wall contractors, 754
Walnut, 755, 834, 1321,
 1322
Warehouse, 756
Warranty, home, 897
Waste
 • hazardous, 541
 • solid, 1235
Water, 757, 1094
 • agencies, 128
 • companies, mutual,
   599
 • environmental
   (pollution), 758
 • groundwater, 538
 • quality, 1117
 • recycled, 1323
 • rural, 666
 • state contractors,
   1269
 • urban, 750
 • works, 128
Weed science, 1356

Welfare directors, 822
Wheat, 759
 • growers, 400
Wild rice, 760
Wine, 101, 127, 1364
 • and food, 85
 • grape growers,
   401, 1011
 • wholesalers, 1363
Winery suppliers, 224
Winemakers, family, 863
Women
 • accountants, 121
 • agriculture, 761
 • architecture, 1365
 • business, 51. 516,
   1366
 • business owners,
   1039, 1040
 • construction, 1041
 • elected, 506
 • film, 1367
 • food service, 1165
 • lawyers, 763
 • timber, 762
Wood products, 1362
Woodwork, 1368
Wool, 764, 1075, 1354
Workers compensation,
765
Writers, 766, 1122,
1373
 • auto racing, 46

–XYZ–

Zoos, 403

CALIFORNIA INSTITUTE OF PUBLIC AFFAIRS

The Institute

The California Institute of Public Affairs, founded in 1969, is an independent, nonprofit, nonpartisan organization affiliated with Claremont Graduate University.

The Institute convenes discussions of leaders and scholars, conducts policy research, and publishes descriptive directories of organizations and information sources. Our work has two dimensions: understanding the character, problems, and future possibilities of California; and improving policy-making on environmental and natural resource problems in California and internationally.

CIPA's special mission is to promote lateral communication and cooperation across professions, academic disciplines, governmental agencies, and other sectors of society. We take no position on political issues; rather, we see our role as a catalyst. We try to help define the public interest by bringing together people with disparate interests to find common ground; bridging the gap between thought and action; and gathering information from a wide variety of sources and translating it into usable form.

Collaborative problem-solving

CIPA organizes collaborative policy forums that bring together leaders and experts who represent different viewpoints and constituencies to try to find agreement on important public issues. These programs include meetings, policy analysis, public outreach, and following up to bring results to decision-makers. Past programs of this kind have concentrated on such issues as energy, agricultural lands, toxic waste, biodiversity, and research for state needs. The Institute has also conducted research and held conferences on the process of collaborative decision-making.

Information guides and reports

The Institute is a leading publisher of information guides on California topics. These include *The*

California Handbook—the standard guide to sources of information about the state—and volumes on government, ethnic groups, environmental protection, water resources, and other topics.

CIPA's research projects and conferences have resulted in reports on such subjects as the public policy process, environmental impact analysis, farmland protection techniques, transportation, and reduction of hazardous waste. A catalog of publications is available on request.

CIPA's offices in downtown Sacramento

International activities

CIPA has been active in international environmental affairs since the early 1970s. Through its International Center for the Environment and Public Policy, the Institute publishes the *World Directory of Environmental Organizations;* works to forge closer links between the study and practice of interdisciplinary approaches to the environment; and promotes exchange of experience in this field between California and foreign countries and international organizations. In recent years, CIPA has been particularly active in Brazil. From 1990-96, the Institute provided the secretariat for the Commission on Environmental Strategy and Planning, part of the International Union for Conservation of Nature and Natural Resources (IUCN - The World Conservation Union).

■

California Institute of Public Affairs
P.O. Box 189040
Sacramento, California 95818
Voice (916) 442-2472 • Fax (916) 442-2478
E-mail cipa@cipahq.org
Web site www.cipahq.org